WORLD PRIEST

BRINGING HEAVEN TO EARTH

MICHAEL MACIEL

BALBOA.
PRESS
A DIVISION OF HAY HOUSE

Balboa Press books may be ordered through booksellers or by contacting:

Balboa Press
A Division of Hay House
1663 Liberty Drive
Bloomington, IN 47403
www.balboapress.com
1 (877) 407-4847

Print information available on the last page.

ISBN: 978-1-5043-3792-2 (sc)
ISBN: 978-1-5043-3793-9 (e)

Balboa Press rev. date: 06/10/2016

For Bernadette

ACKNOWLEDGMENTS

Descriptions of the Priesthood are as numerous and varied as those about parenthood, science, and literature. But it's within the multiplicity of opinions that we can find our own interpretations of this crucial part of the spiritual path and perhaps find new openings to explore in our search for greater understanding.

There are those who provided such openings for me. Earl W. Blighton (Father Paul), Director General of the Holy Order of MANS, and Helen Blighton (Mother Ruth), Co-director, are the two primary influences in my life. I am and shall always be indebted to them for my spiritual training and well-being.

I would also like to thank Timothy Harris and Jessika Lucas for their kind and patient support over the years and for showing me by their example how to help others find their unique path to God.

And to my many friends in the Way: Matthias Dominic Indra, Rosamonde Miller, John Plummer, David Lowell,

Sarah Beckett, Ann and Robert Drucker, Josephine Shaffer, Tamzon and Charles Askren, Mark Earlix, Shawn Collins, Margo and Hamid Emami, Lenore Flanders, Mary Ann Fry, Grace Tin-Yen Christus, Beatrice Borden, Cynthia Coate-Ray, Andrew Shykofsky, Clare Watts, Mary Christopher, Mary Francis Drake and many, many others who have supported me in my work throughout the years.

And thanks to Paula Gillen of Gillen Edits for her beautiful cover art, both for *World Priest* and *The Five Vows*.

Ultimately there are no paths. There is only the Way, which is universal. We all have a personal and unique connection with the One Self, which requires no intercession, no intermediaries. But we may find it helpful to align ourselves with a strain of consciousness, a stream of transformative power, force and energy that has been trod by countless others throughout time. Those are the paths that lead us to that experience of our unique connection with the One. And we benefit from that living stream and from all who are "above" as they extend a helping hand to us, to help us ascend that ladder of initiation.

– Matthias Dominic Indra

INTRODUCTION

I was in the Joslyn Art Museum in Omaha, Nebraska, standing in front of a Monet. It was a huge canvas—water lilies on a pond—that must have measured ten feet across, or so it seemed. I was feeling a little impatient that day, and looking at this vast expanse of blue green wasn't helping. I mean, what *is* the point? The only impression I was getting was that either Monet needed glasses or he needed painting lessons, or perhaps both. So I thought I'd listen to the recording device that I had picked up in the lobby to see if there was something I was missing.

The voice in the recording told me what I wasn't seeing. It said that what was remarkable about this painting wasn't the lilies or the pond. What was remarkable was the reflection of the sky in the water. I almost fell over. All of a sudden, I was looking through the painting at the sky. The canvas became a window, and it showed me a sky that was more real than any sky I had ever seen before. It was thrilling. The blue was such that I could sense the air, and the surface of the water invisible enough that I could feel its coolness on my face. And the lilies? Mere bystanders. It was the sky, the sun-drenched sky, a sky that with its whitewashed brilliance let me know that the world is a very big place, and its bigness was being reflected back to me through this tiny opening in the surface of the pond.

Had I not been told what to look for, I might never have seen it. My impatience had been with my own blindness, a blindness of which I was unaware. But the paintings in the museum seemed to know that I was blind, that I wasn't *seeing them*, and they weren't going to let me leave without hearing what they had to say. And what they were saying was *WAKE UP!*

So it is with the presence of God in the world. We live in a sea of presence. It is all around us, extending outwards into infinity. It also extends within us, reaching just as far. And here we are on the cusp, our own personal event horizon, negotiating, reconciling, trying to interpret one within the context of the other, looking first out there and then within, wondering which of these two worlds is more vast. Yet the power of the presence persists, sometimes drawing us into the beauty of the world, and sometimes into the dark luminescence of the inner cave of our soul.

Such is our entry point into the world of the real. Previously, we thought we knew the world, gauging it by the measure of our eyes and the parameters of our understanding, but now we see it as though for the first time, and we marvel at how we missed it. The span of our life as we have known it seems truncated, as though it were only now just beginning—a second birth—turning everything that went before into a dream. We stand on a threshold, one that is unlike anything we have experienced, beyond which is something that beckons us with irresistible force, a power that is both intimate and infinite, close and incredibly far, wider than the sky and yet able to fit within the chambers of our heart.

This is the awakening. It is an experience that everyone has had or will have, either sooner or later. And it is this awakening that sets one on the spiritual path. There are those for whom this path is a way to improve their lives, to make them more sensitive to others, to be more forgiving, or to be more trusting of the universe, so that life is better for them, more fulfilling, and more meaningful. They find peace within themselves and are thus able to live more peacefully with others and with the world. It makes them more productive while at the same time less attached. They feel free, perhaps for the first time in their life. There is no greater feeling, no deeper satisfaction than to be alive in the moment and to be in sync with the world.

But there are others for whom no amount of satisfaction will suffice, for whom the world is not enough—can never be enough—to bring them peace. Perhaps this is where you find yourself now. For you, it is as though there is a fire within you, and that fire will never let you rest until you find its source. It is a fire that drives you away from the safety of the familiar and into dangerous places, places that harbor unknown worlds and unknown powers, places that seem to be hidden behind a curtain that is simultaneously diaphanous and impenetrable—a veil translucent with an invisible light, a dark radiance that is both intelligent and alive. No amount of worldly pleasure or familial love is enough to dissuade your thorough investigation of this unknown, unseeable *something* that insists that you find it, that you give it your undivided attention and that you be *willing* to hear what it has to say.

As you get more comfortable in your inner space, you begin to judge outer sources of wisdom by how closely they resonate with this inner light, by how well they help to strip away the distractions of the mind and heart and thus bring that which is behind the veil closer to you or you closer to it. Ideas and philosophies start to wane in their importance. Theories no longer impress. It's *practice* that you're after now, and no amount of thinking, reading, or debating will substitute for it. You're only interested in that which will take you farther within, deeper into the Well of Souls that lies hidden under the massive weight of your materialistic way of life.

And the more you pursue it, the less able you are to function day to day. Your outer circumstances begin to fall apart. What worked before no longer does, and you start to feel like the world is a foreign place in which you no longer fit. It is the flight of the alone to the alone, and a tighter passageway there has never been. But you persist. You go deeper and deeper within, spending hours, sometimes days in meditation, turning away from all outer distractions, probing the depths of your own awareness. What is life when there is no "out there"? There at the end of your rope, in the face of utter failure, in the stark realization that there is no meaning to anything and that everything you thought you knew is false, you hit bottom. And for the first time in your life, you feel like you are finally standing on solid ground. Empty of opinion, stripped of striving, denied all recognition and acceptance by others, you are empty. And in that emptiness your eyes are opened, and you see for the first time life as it really is—present, immediate, unrelenting, a force like no other, a force that both moves the world and holds it in its place. And in that realization, a light bursts in. Your body becomes filled with light, and the power and energy of the cosmos becomes the very life of your body, and you understand, perhaps for the first time, what eternal life really is.

In the days following, everything looks different, feels different, and responds in new ways. All of your seeking has brought you to this place, and you feel as though you have been born anew. You look around and you are amazed that no one else can see what you are seeing. The things that you once held important still captivate everyone you see. They seem totally distracted by the unreal, as though they were chasing shadows on the ground. Your heart begins to open to them, not in pity but in true compassion, and you begin the long process of learning how to serve your fellow human beings. You look for ways to get through to them, how to slowly turn their gaze upwards, how to wrench their desires away from objects and onto God, which for them at this point in their development can only be a concept.

You teach. You help. You find ways to heal their insanity, to open their eyes so that they can see the real world that is all around them, the one they cannot see with their physical eyes. For those who are convinced that the world they see is the only world that exists, you simply have to give them room to play out their dramas. They may be good people, but they're not ready to let go of the world. So for them, your teaching is inappropriate. It could even be harmful. Rather, you look for those who have begun to suspect that there is more to life than meets the eye, that there are meanings and experiences that can only be reached within themselves, people who are where you once were—driven by an insatiable desire to an unknown, interior destination. These are the ones you now dedicate yourself to serve. It's not that the others are unworthy; they're just not ready. Their current lesson is to master the world—to learn how to think, to develop earthly skills, to perfect the body—not to leave it. So, don't interfere with their curriculum. You've already learned those lessons. Your job now is to integrate that knowledge into your new awareness, to bring Earth to heaven, and then later, heaven to Earth.

This is what it means to be a priest. One part of you is in heaven and the other part is in the world. You span the two. You are the bridge between the world of God and the world of nature, the universal and the particular, the macrocosm and the microcosm. If you use your spiritual experience to escape the world, you cannot be a priest. That's not what priests do. To be a priest, you must be *in the world*. But while you are in the world, your direction comes from within. It comes from the God in you—your Divine Self—the part of you that is made in the image and likeness of the Nameless One. And everything you do is for the sake of the world—its life, its vitality, its intelligence, its capacity to love. These qualities do not come from the world itself; they come from above. You may not be perfect (no one ever is), but you must be able to *access* perfection. And that you *can* do.

So let's begin this work of accessing perfection. Each of the following chapters covers a different aspect of life and reality as it pertains to the spiritual path. It's not a complete list, but it's a good place to start. The concepts you encounter here are like building blocks, each one adapted to a particular purpose. None are sufficient by themselves. No single one can form the basis of a complete philosophy. But together, they form a good foundation upon which you can build your life of service. If questions arise, I encourage you to take them into meditation. Let them work on your consciousness in their own time. Take them with you when you go to sleep at night, and let them reveal themselves. Because what we are dealing with here is reality, which is far greater than any human mind can comprehend, nor can it be articulated. *But it can be known!* This book will give you everything you need in order to build a framework within which true knowing can emerge—*in you*. And that's where it counts, is it not?

CONTENTS

PART 1

ARE YOU A PRIEST?

CHAPTER 1

ARE YOU A PRIEST?

At some point in everyone's spiritual evolution, they will feel a shift. Perhaps you have felt it already. It feels like moving from one room to another or from one house to another. The world looks different, and you are no longer the person you once were. We go through many such transitions throughout the course of our lives, but this is different. It's not simply a rite of passage in the process of growing up, nor is it a change in the way we relate to society. This is a rite of passage of the soul. And once it happens, it cannot be undone.

In a secular sense, a priest is a functionary of a spiritual tradition, which makes it difficult to envision the Priesthood outside of a religious context. But the Priesthood is more than what society has made of it. It is more than religions have made of it. Rather than an institutional office, the Priesthood is a spiritual state of being. It's about our relationship with God—our *direct* relationship with God—not our relationship with God through society or an institution. And although God perhaps expresses through us best when we interact with each other in love, we do not derive the substance of that love from each other, but rather through our individual connection with the Divine.

The Priesthood *is* that individual connection. As such, it exists, at least potentially, within every person.

Do you feel estranged from religion? Do you find it increasingly difficult to see other human beings as spiritually superior (or inferior)? Are the Scriptures—any of them—starting to feel less relevant in your life? These are signs that your relationship with God is changing, that it's becoming more direct and less dependent upon a go-between. Why else would more and more people describe themselves as spiritual but not religious? In this book, we will explore this primary relationship, our *inner* Priesthood, and we will look at ways to maximize our effectiveness in the world.

The world has plenty of ministers, just as there are plenty of social workers. But priests are not necessarily social workers, nor do all priests work in the ministry. Does this surprise you? Conventionally speaking, priests *are* ministers; they are social workers. They provide counseling, they build spiritual communities, and they work for peace and justice for the world at large. But these activities, as noble and necessary as they are, do not define the Priesthood.

Neither do the sacraments, which are indeed part and parcel of the Priesthood, define it, especially when they are performed merely as church rituals, which makes them proprietary functions only. If they are only performed at an altar, a wedding, a hospital bed, or in the confessional, then they are not exclusive to the Priesthood. Any minister could do as much. But there is a larger context to the Priesthood and the sacraments, larger than the context of church activities. Much larger.

Let's take this idea of the priesthood one step further. If a priest doesn't have to be a minister, if the priesthood is not confined to ordinary ideas of religion or spirituality, then anyone, regardless of their profession or station in life, can be a priest. A priest can be a doctor or a scientist, a school teacher or a stay-at-home mom. He can be the guy who sells hot dogs on the street corner or a politician campaigning for re-election. Even your plumber (I know several plumbers who are priests) or the contractor building an addition onto the back of your house can be a priest. Any of these people can be a priest and not necessarily serve as a minister in a church.

The priesthood is not restricted to occupational boundaries and definitions. Every area of human endeavor adds in some way to the advancement of human consciousness, and they all benefit from having priests in their ranks. As priests, we live and work *in the world*; total immersion is the very definition of the Incarnation. But it's hard to be in the world if you live in an ivory tower. Ivory towers can include ideologies, beliefs, and sectarian identities. Priests are mediators between God and humanity, not just purveyors of ideas. Ideas are empty without the Spirit of God moving through them, so unless a priest can mediate *that*, their ideas will be largely ineffective.

If you're wondering who out there might be an *incognito* priest, it's easy enough to spot them. Just look at the cutting edge of any profession; look for the people who are in it because they *have to be* and not just for money or fame. Look for those who knew since they were children that they *had* to be a doctor, a teacher, an artist, a musician, a writer, a filmmaker. Look for those who are seized by their vision, who could not walk away from their chosen work if you put a gun to their head. (Perhaps you feel that way about your own work.) Look for those people whose work produces changes in the world, changes that might not necessarily appear constructive but are nonetheless pivotal. Look for the game changers, the revolutionaries, those whose actions have not only changed people›s lives, but the context in which they live them.

And once you've drawn up your list, try to imagine that these shining examples are but the tip of the iceberg. There are legions of others who work quietly behind the scenes, the ones who provide the prayer support for their brothers and sisters on the front lines, the ones whose mission it is to take a public stand, perhaps risking their lives for the changes they champion.

Any time we find an individual who feels called to actively advance the spiritual well-being of mankind, we are likely looking at a priest. Amongst historical figures, there are many examples: Benjamin Franklin, George Washington, Marie Curie, Nikola Tesla, and Mother Jones, to name a few. Farther in the past, there were Pythagoras, Plato, Socrates, Hypatia of Alexandria, Paracelsus, and Queen Elizabeth I. More recently, we have people such as Rosa Parks, Martin Luther King (though some might see him as more of a religious leader), Ralph Nader, and Benazir Bhutto, the first woman to head the government of an Islamic state. Some of these examples are scientists, some are political leaders, and some are reformers. None, with the exception of King, were clergy. And though they might not have regarded *themselves* as priests, they all advanced the spiritual consciousness of people everywhere. They were spiritual leaders whose effects reached far beyond their goals. Their life missions were seemingly powered by a force greater than themselves, ordained, as it were, by a Higher Power. And that power manifested itself in them as an authority of a definitively spiritual nature.

One does not need to be a great public figure in order to be a priest. Even though such people have influenced history and affected the lives of millions of people, God knows nothing about scale. "There is no great and no small to the mind that maketh all," said Ralph Waldo Emerson. A single act of forgiveness made with the consciousness of the presence of God could end a war or heal a nation. A simple question asked within the Holy of Holies of one's own being could provide the cure for a disease or inspire the world's most beautiful work of art. We never know for certain what the outcome of our actions will be, but when in the course of our daily activities we carry the Presence of God, we make possible the transformation of the planet.

Priests heal the world. Sounds grandiose, does it not? Who, after all, is worthy to assume such a task? Surely, the only people who would be interested would be egomaniacs and sociopaths, eager to assume power over others, attracted to any high-sounding title that holds the promise of such power. But this is not what we are interested in. This is not what our calling is about. If you have a calling to the Priesthood, and it is genuine, then you know instinctively that it is a calling to serve—to serve God by serving *all* of humanity in its spiritual needs.

CHAPTER 2

THE ONE MIND

We have to recognize that Earth's problems are *mental*. They will not go away until the destructive mindsets that got us into this mess are corrected. And while it's true that we must be actively transforming our minds before we can transform the minds of others, it is *not* true that the world changes only one person at a time. There are many ways to *leverage* our ability to change the One Mind, raising our powers of influence to exponential levels. Collectively, these methods are known as "priestcraft," and they are the main topic of this book.

So, what is the "One Mind"? It is the combined thinking of everyone on this planet, an energized medium to which our brains are attuned. It is the repository of the thought patterns that have been put there since the dawn of humanity. And although we are the ones who created the One Mind, it in turn has recreated us. Our brains' neural architecture reflects the thought patterns in the One Mind. We put them there by our thinking, collectively and individually, both past and present.

Our physical brains are the manifestation of the One Mind. They are one of the most advanced mechanisms by which the world processes information about itself. The thoughts we think are the thoughts we are *prone* to think, their inclinations coming from both our genetics and the energies that fill the space around us. Our thoughts generate these energies and in turn are generated by them. The more we think certain thoughts, the more likely we are to continue thinking them.

Everyone is a broadcasting station. We continually send forth our thoughts, charged with our feelings, into the collective mind of the world in which we live. The depth of our connection with each other is profound, each of us affecting the other with the quality of our spiritual presence. But if the broadcast we send forth is merely the sum of our human experiences, we only reinforce what is already there.

The Priesthood is about adding something new to the mix, thoughts and energies of a higher origin, energies that by their very presence will transform the world. Priests, *real* priests (which anyone can be regardless of their religion, education, or station in life) have the power to think *new* thoughts energized by the Spirit of God. Having raised their consciousness above the noise of the One Mind and having broken free of the automatism of instinctual thinking, they are capable of introducing new ideas and new spiritual energies into the collective consciousness of the world.

We are all aware of this aspect of human existence—the sea of consciousness wherein we live out our lives. Moments of synchronicity, though usually taking us by surprise, nonetheless feel right. They feel as though the universe knows our every move, orchestrating events according to the strength of our convictions and the clarity of our intentions. We seem drawn to people and places that hold meaning for us, that give us opportunities to grow and to feel connected.

This field of consciousness—the One Mind—is the real geography, the terrain we navigate every day of our lives. Its deep currents act upon us with relentless power, unaffected by the ever-changing weather of superficial opinion. The One Mind is the real world in which we live, not the world of politics, economics, or even religious ideology. Our innermost feelings and convictions float in this vast open sea like icebergs on the ocean, oblivious to the winds that blow fiercely upon them, harnessed instead to the unseen currents in which they are entrained.

Becoming aware of the real world of the One Mind is just the first step in realizing our power to affect the world around us. When we see that our thoughts are continuously broadcasting into a collective medium, we start to pay attention to the quality of our thinking. What are we contributing? When we ask ourselves this question, self-knowledge and self-observation become very important, and a new sense of responsibility begins to emerge within us. We begin to realize that we are indeed either part of the solution or part of the problem. What we speak to ourselves in the enclosure of our self-awareness is shouted from the rooftops within the One Mind.

As a medium, the One Mind is neutral; it takes on the predominant characteristics of the thoughts we think into it. The kind of person we are and how we treat our fellow human beings—not just physically, but mentally as well—influence the spiritual quality of the One Mind. Thoughts of retribution, feelings of resentment, anger, jealousy, and lust, as well as thoughts of compassion, community, and generosity—these all affect the One Mind, and by extension they affect every other human being.

The way people think becomes the way they are likely to think, because we tend to think the thoughts that are already present in the One Mind. The problems of the world will reflect themselves in our thinking—not because we adopt them, but because they are already present in the collective consciousness of the world.

Because of this propensity to think what has already been thought, we quickly realize that anything we add to this collective mind can only be more of what is already there, and so our efforts at changing it start to feel woefully insufficient. We begin to look for grace, something higher and purer than what we are, something that can truly raise the vibration of the collective mind out of its never-ending feedback loop. We draw our thoughts from the One Mind the same way we draw water from a well, but how can we make a difference if the water we add is as polluted as the well we draw it from? Instinctively, we look up with our spiritual eyes and search the heavens for grace—that unconditional rain that falls on the just and unjust alike.

We pray to God for help. We ask for light to illuminate us, so that what shines forth from within us can heal this collective consciousness. We look for opportunities to help those in need, and as we connect with others, we begin to see that what we do to one person, we do to everyone, including ourselves. Such is the nature of this interconnected sea of consciousness in which we live.

We spend years seeking ways to be of service to people, looking for ways to help them turn *their* spiritual eyes upward, so that they too might receive grace from God. We discover that it really doesn't matter what outer form our service takes; it only matters that we perform it with love, which is to say that we perform our acts of service with a high degree of intention and with the *knowing* that we are all connected through the One Mind. It's our knowing—our conviction and our confidence—that forms the operational basis of our priestly authority. And, it's our connection with all that lives that allows it to work. Anyone who develops this connection can be a priest, regardless of who they are or what they have done. God is no respecter of persons. In other words, *God doesn't care* who you are, only that you are willing to help.

Whether we are the abbot of an ashram, a parish priest, a social worker, a barista at Starbucks, or a convicted felon, we can all be a channel of service to people everywhere. All that's required is that we do not lose our connection with humanity. After all, to love is to stay connected. We must never separate ourselves from *anyone*, regardless of how depraved or "evil" they seem, because we all have the capacity for evil to one degree or another. To separate ourselves from evil people (in other words, to *judge* them) only increases the likelihood that we will become evil ourselves. Why? Because the problem does not lie within the other person; the problem lies within the One Mind.

Opposing the problem only strengthens it. So doing away with evil people solves nothing. Their hatred and prejudice will survive in the One Mind long after they are dead. Hatred and prejudice thrive on separation, but they dissipate wherever there is connection.

As we observe our own thoughts, we cannot help but realize that everything we think comes from the collective consciousness we call the One Mind. And it is only when we become conscious of this fact that we are able to offer our minds to God as a conduit for something new. When we see that the chatter in our heads is not our own but rather the background noise of the One Mind, we are able, perhaps for the first time, to see past those thoughts into the Mind of God. It is from *that* mind that all good things come.

CHAPTER 3

WHERE DO PRIESTS COME FROM?

While the laying on of hands and the oral transmission of sacred teachings is a necessary part of a spiritual heritage, realistically it is not the only way the priesthood is handed down. Sometimes, as in the case of Saint Paul on the road to Damascus, people are ordained directly by the heavenly Host, without the mediation of a physical teacher or recognized lineage. The trouble with the word "lineage" is that it is so *linear*, time-wise—who gave what to whom and when they gave it. We have to look at the concept of "lineage" from a different perspective, because we cannot understand spiritual things with a mundane mind.

The word "lineage" derives from the word "line." So does the word "align." Let us suppose then that lineage has more to do with alignment than it does with history. But what we are talking about is not necessarily an alignment of doctrine or belief. Rather, it is an alignment of consciousness, energy, and will—a *spiritual* alignment. One preserves a tradition; the other advances a spiritual movement. The American Hindu master, Subramuniya, said that awareness, energy, and will are all one and the same thing. People (meaning both men and women) of Good Will, of high consciousness, and who use energy in positive, life-affirming ways are automatically in alignment with each other. Therefore, they are of the same *lineage*—they are of one *spirit*.

Spiritual unity is not necessarily intellectual unity. We can have widely divergent opinions about religion, morals, ethics, and politics, and we can still be aligned in our will, our consciousness, and our energy. This is the "rock" upon which we build our church. What does it matter if we are saved by works or by grace? To the intellect, these concepts are *very* important, but not to the Spirit. Because in reality, our understanding of these things falls far short of the truth. Our cherished concepts are likely to be limited, since the intellect is the smallest sliver of our being. Spiritual truth is spiritual, not intellectual.

When we worship together in Spirit, ritual and law take a backseat to the intention we hold as we approach the Almighty. It is possible, therefore, for a Muslim, a Christian, a Jew, and a Buddhist to worship together at the same altar *if* they worship in a unified spirit. But, the moment doctrinal differences are brought in, unity dissolves and dissension begins. The Spirit is lost. When we build our faith on intellectual ground, we place ourselves farthest away from Divinity, because we make the intellect the final judge of truth, which it is not equipped to be. Only Spirit can discern Spirit, and the intellect is not Spirit.

If lineage means the alignment of consciousness, energy, and will, then it is no longer dependent on time. It exists in the present moment. This means that we can step into and out of it at any time. We are like radios that are either tuned in or tuned out. Lineage is not historical, is not time-bound, and only exists in the now. Spiritual lineage is based in Spirit, not in tradition.

Having said this, I do believe (because I have experienced it) that a time stamp does take place at an ordination. But it's an energetic time-stamp, not a corporate stamp embossed on a piece of paper. By "time-stamp," I mean that something happens in that moment, something that *cannot be undone*. Something is inscribed on the initiate's soul. That "something" becomes true north for that person, a kind of recalibration of his or her spirit. How? By dedicating ourselves to God in service through the Priesthood, heaven dedicates itself to us, bringing us under its mantle, and we are changed forever.

As initiations, Priesthood ordinations have a kind of lens effect, the way a magnifying glass focuses sunlight to set a piece of paper on fire. They're set up to focus and concentrate awareness, willpower, and energy—the "one thing" described by Subramuniya. Of course, the person performing the rite must first be in alignment with the Host above, the heavenly convocation of masters who serve God by helping us in our spiritual evolution. Otherwise, it becomes merely a ceremony conferring organizational authority only.

Because lineage has to do with the alignment of spiritual qualities and not religious affiliation or adherence to a specific doctrine, priests operating in different religions or fields of service can be of the same lineage. This is the true brotherhood of priests. It does not matter if one is Christian or Buddhist, Muslim or Hindu, or even spiritual or secular. If the same spirit is at work, it's the same lineage. Again, we cannot understand spiritual things with a mundane mind. And we cannot equate a spiritual state of being with the appointed office of a man-made organization.

Chapter 4

The Sanctity of Life

If we are to move past the differences that divide us as a world spiritual community, we have to look first at those things that unite us. All religions, at least those that have persisted over time, hold that life is sacred. We take this for granted. But if this is a core principle in the world's enduring religions, we need to examine it more closely and find out for ourselves what "sanctity of life" really means.

One thing that science has taught us is that all life on Earth is interdependent. Each species is a strand in the larger web we call the biosphere. Pluck one strand and the whole web vibrates. But the true relationships between the various species of plants, animals, and humans is scarcely known, because science only looks at the outer forms of life and not at the life *power* that runs through them. It views the phenomenon of life as a biochemical reaction and not as the self-expression of a multi-faceted, universal, intelligent Being.

Science understands how electricity works, but it sees life like an electrician who can only see wires, not the energies flowing through them. It sees the life energy of each different species as though it were a separate house in a neighborhood that somehow generates its own electricity from vats of chemicals in the basement, rather than by being connected to a larger electrical grid. Until science learns that life derives its "force" from one fundamental frequency and then divides itself into a harmony of individualized expressions, it cannot understand the true basis of life's interdependence within itself. And until it does this, the idea that life is sacred will forever remain a mystery to science.

Science has also taught us that all life evolves. Hermes, the ancient philosopher and scientist who predated the scientific era by several thousands of years, said in his *Emerald Tablet* that God, the "One Thing," gives birth to all things out of Itself through adaptation. Never was there a clearer statement of the meaning of evolution. But modern science sees this adaptation as the result of a random selection of successful adaptive traits, a *competition* among species for their own perpetuation. Hermes, however, saw it as Spirit's *exploration* of the multitudinous possibilities of its own Self-expression. The one sees winners and losers, the other only one winner—the entire system of life on this planet.

Hermes shows us that the One Thing introverted upon Itself in a kind of cosmic cell-division for the purpose of giving birth to its own divine image. The goal of this creative act was to set in motion the fullest possible realization of

Its own potential. And in order for this exploration to be successful, there had to be built-in harmonies to ensure that the whole thing didn't fly apart. This inherent harmony was a given, because the One Thing had nothing else to work with but Itself. Lacking discord, It could not create it. Thus came about the harmonious and hugely diverse system of life on Earth.

Evolution is not a contest for dominance but rather a symphony of interrelated expressions of the One Life. If it were a contest for dominance, at the end there could only be one species left, which for a *system* would be utterly unworkable. The goal of evolution, therefore, is one of greater and greater diversity, not less.

It is inevitable, however, that as the greater system builds upon itself, some individual forms outlive their intended purposes and are removed, just as we strip away the plywood forms from the hardened concrete of the foundation of a new house. The individual form is demolished, but the life within the form is not. The life within the form is the One Life, "the same force that through the green fuse drives the flower," as the poet Dylan Thomas described it. It cannot be destroyed. You can't even say that it is diverted, because the One Life does not move; it simply *is*. It manifests the forms it needs and then sloughs them off when they are no longer needed (Kali and Kala of Hindu mythology). It is the *forms* that come into being and go out of being; the One Life remains forever.

But for the One Life to flourish in its multitudinous Self-expressions, it needs a viable and sustainable planetary system through which to work. The system is the important thing, not the forms. Therefore, anything that threatens the health of the system undermines its form-creating capabilities. A good example of this is the acidification of the world's oceans, brought on by the increased levels of carbon dioxide that it absorbs from the atmosphere. The ocean's increased acidity is adversely affecting coral reefs, dissolving the calcium in their calcium carbonate structures. Coral reefs provide the habitat for twenty-five percent of all the world's marine species. Disrupt it and you undermine the food chain itself. The ocean is the primary component of the planet's ecosystem. Change it and you alter the entire biosphere. Any act against it is a blatant disregard for the sanctity of life.

The One Life expresses itself in an autonomic way— it is conscious, but it is not self-conscious. It knows *how* to do everything, but it cannot choose to do anything except that which is demanded by the perfect logic of its universal interconnectivity. The precision of its inherent intelligence enables it to adapt its forms to an ever-changing environment. Nature is ruthless in its adaptations; its networks are programmed to maximize its own long-term viability.

Whereas Nature is selflessly intelligent, humanity is just the opposite. Humanity's sense of *self* is dominant, while its eco-intelligence operates in isolation from the whole. We have to figure out how to adapt to our environment, whereas nature exercises its powers of adaptability automatically. This limitation on our part is simultaneously a blessing and a curse. It enables us to survive and thrive in hostile environments, greatly expanding our possibilities. But, it also makes it hard for us to tell when our actions are harming the system, because the results of our actions often take decades or even centuries to make themselves obvious.

Fire is the symbol for the One Life. As a living symbol, the use of fire in a temple represents the presence of the One Life in the innermost chamber of the human body. The Priesthood is the keeper of this eternal flame. It is the priests of the world—the *world* priests—who keep the flame alive by communing with it and by using it to heal the world. Keeping in mind that the One Life is also intelligent, this eternal flame is a world priests' source of wisdom.

> *Maybe a great magnet pulls*
> *All souls towards truth*
> *Or maybe it is life itself*
> *Feeds wisdom to its youth*
> – from Constant Craving, sung by K.D. Lang

The power, force, and energy of the One Life is intelligent by its very nature, and it manifests its own forms of expression through activity, which is also its nature. This is expressed in mystical language as Will, Wisdom, and Activity. The three act together. They are, in fact, *the* Holy Trinity, symbolized by an equilateral triangle. The triangle has to be equilateral, because these three elements—Will, Wisdom, and Activity—are the three aspects of the "One Thing" spoken of by Hermes. Take away any one of them, and the other two disappear. This is why some branches of the Christian faith say that Father, Son, and Holy Spirit are co-equal, co-eternal, and co-substantial.

God is conscious. God has a soul (in Hinduism called *Akasha*). This is why we sometimes see the equilateral triangle with an eye at the center or, as on the dollar bill, suspended above it. God is capable of *seeing* and *hearing* and *feeling*—all attributes of personhood. Without this understanding, realizing our oneness with God would be impossible. This is why most of Christianity insists that Father, Son, and Holy Spirit are *persons*. God is more than an impersonal force.

The eye in the triangle indicates that we are sentient beings. If we start with the premise that we are *already* one with God and that our seeming separation from God is an illusion (or a dream from which we awaken), then we can understand why the Bible says that the Son of God (*us*) is begotten and not made. We are *extensions* of God, just as children are extensions of their parents. Parents don't "make" their children the way they make a loaf of bread. Children are begotten. Children are sentient beings. Children are *persons.*

The idea that God is a person is perhaps the single most important contribution by religion to our collective consciousness. Without it, we could not help but come to the conclusion that we are merely bio-mechanical machines. Persons, in the understanding of religion, have a soul—a memory that lives above and beyond our physical selves. It *survives* us. It's the part of us created by God, which in mystical language means that it's the real part of us, the part that never dies. Within it dwells the Spirit of God shining with the power of the great spiritual Sun, and together they comprise who we *are* as individuals.

Through this simple concept that God is a person, we get all of our notions of human rights, especially the rights of individuals. This is what distinguishes the Western

Esoteric Tradition—its emphasis on the sanctity of life of the *individual.* Heretofore, we have talked about the sanctity of life-*systems,* placing the interests of the Whole above the interests of individual forms. So it's important to understand the true nature of human life in the full spectrum of its spiritual reality. We are the Self (the indwelling Spirit of God) wearing first the sheath of the soul (that which makes us an individual) and secondly the sheath of flesh, called the physical body.

What makes human life sacred is not the physical body; it is the Self and soul of the individual. If the body were the spiritual part of us, then its needs and concerns would constitute our highest spiritual ideal. But just as Jesus told us not to fear those who can kill the body but rather to fear those who can torment the soul, so must we comprehend our life as a spiritual expression in a physical environment. We use the physical body as our vehicle of expression, not as the seat of our identity. Unless we live our lives in this context, we quickly come to see ourselves as a phenomenon of nature only, and we start to live our lives according to its rules, which by and large are those of a machine, governed solely by the law of cause and effect.

When we subordinate life to the law of cause and effect, we invent all sorts of misguided and deformed ideas of morality and justice. These ideas include karma (as punishment), guilt, fear, and the caste system (which insidiously finds its way into *all* cultures). Mercy and compassion are the first things to go, because sin *must* be punished—the law of cause and effect demands it. By placing ourselves under the dominion of nature, we destroy any sense of the rights of individuals. We abdicate our power to establish a rule of law, self-government, and the freedom to develop our human potential. Might becomes right—the stronger rule the weaker—and exploitation becomes the norm. Individual human lives become *expendable*. People cease being citizens and become *consumers* instead. We give up our personhood and become commodities to be bought and sold.

Saying that we should not subordinate ourselves to nature is not intended to denigrate nature in any way. Nature is beautiful, but we have distanced ourselves from it in ways that work against us, which has perhaps more than anything else blinded us to the beauty in ourselves.

Life is sacred not simply because we are alive but because the life in us is bigger than we are. It is the One Life. We are individual expressions of the Spirit of God, which manifests itself here on the Earth plane through activity. As we connect and reconnect with the One Life, it transmits itself into our spiritual and physical bodies, and then, through us, finds its way into the rest of the natural world. We are the go-betweens. How do we know this? Just look at what our activities are doing to the biosphere. We have the power of life and death over creation, and unfortunately we are on a killing spree. So many species (*systems*) are dying that scientists are calling our era the Second Great Extinction. The first one was 65 million years ago when an asteroid wiped out the dinosaurs and most of the other species of animals. Our impact on the biosphere is so significant that geologists are saying that we have entered into a new geological era, and they're naming it after us: the Anthropocene Era. This time, *we* are the asteroid.

This is why we say that the Priesthood is greater than any sectarian religion. The Priesthood is real and eternal; religion is man-made. The Priesthood is as essential to life on Earth as the pineal gland is to the health of the human body. The Priesthood makes communication between heaven and Earth possible. Without it, this planet would be cut off from the rest of creation.

The sanctity of life is the coat of arms of the Priesthood, its *raison d'etre*. At once both passionate and dispassionate, the priests of God maintain this connection with the One Life with ruthless integrity, and it is through the Priesthood that life on Earth preserves its momentum in its never-ending exploration of its own potential.

World priests are the protectors of life on Earth. Their chief concern is for *all* of life, not just the lives of their family, their friends, or their country. They serve all families, all people everywhere, and all nations. They accept everyone as they are and are not swept up in any public vilification of other groups or countries. They do not *demonize* the other. They realize that diversity is the best insurance for the long-term viability of the human race, so they do not judge on the basis of appearances alone.

Each country has its own spiritual current, its own unique contribution to the diversity of the spiritual expression of the One Life as it explores the possibilities of its own potential here on Earth. It stands to reason that some of those expressions are going to look diametrically opposed to each other. Some are going to find it very difficult to peacefully coexist without a sizeable buffer zone between them. But, isn't this the case within our own physical bodies? The acid in our stomachs serves an important role in digestion, but that same acid would quickly destroy its surrounding tissues only millimeters away. This proves that diversity depends on healthy boundaries in order to work for the success of the whole. This does not mean that some groups need to be segregated from the rest. No. When people develop healthy boundaries, they don't need to remove themselves from society. Instead, both they and the society in which they live learn to respect each other's differences. They don't try to force each other to conform.

Being a world priest does not mean that everyone should worship God in the same way, or that nations should all blend into one superstate. That would not only be impractical, it would be dangerous as well. For the One Life to find the harmonies inherent within its own being, there must be separate, distinct notes with which to build its chords. Just as music depends on a diversity of notes and measures, so does life on this planet depend on the integrity and viability of each individual species.

"Sanctity of life" has a deeper meaning than simply "all life is sacred." Just having a pulse doesn't make you holy. We must be rigorously loyal to our own kind *and* be uncompromising in our protection of the rights of others to exist, even when their form of life-expression is dramatically different from our own. It doesn't mean we have to like them; it means that we have to *respect* them. Real love does not demand that we like those who are different from us, but it always demands our respect.

Chapter 5

The Presence of a Higher Intelligence

After the Sanctity of Life, the second basic principle found in all religions and that can therefore unite the priests of different traditions is the presence of a higher intelligence that creates and sustains the world. It recognizes that the One Life is informed by thought and is not merely a blind force. Whereas science opts to go with the blind force model, the mystically-inclined person sees life as imbued with intelligence and motivated by love.

As with the sanctity of life, world priests have to look at this principle of the presence of a higher intelligence with modern eyes. We have to expand our definition of "mind" and also our definition of "intelligence." The following is a model that can give us a way to understand these important principles:

Any place we observe interconnectivity, we are observing mind. And the action that takes place within those interconnections is intelligence.

In order to make sense of this model, we have to de-anthropomorphize the terms "mind" and "intelligence" and see them instead as universal phenomena of nature. Everything has its own specific coding that holds it in its shape and determines its range of action and interaction. The type of body we have is determined by our genetic code; the way one chemical interacts with another chemical is determined by its valence; jigsaw puzzles are governed by the shapes of their pieces. We use the word "thinking" (a word which is not well understood) to describe the *process* by which codes interact.

The word "brain" is another word that is not well understood. We take it for granted that all brains have to look roughly the same, that they must all have the same form-factor. But in reality, we can call any system of nodes that has a high degree of interconnectivity a brain. And the activity within that interconnectivity is that brain's intelligence. The more nodes there are—especially when they are grouped into complex systems—the more intelligence there is. When the interactions become extremely complex, we say that the system acts *intelligently*.

Scientists have discovered that plants exhibit behavior. They asked the obvious question: how can plants exhibit behavior when they don't have a brain? They concluded that the brain of a plant species is spread out over its entire population. Each individual plant is a neuron in that brain. It communicates with the other members of the network through its roots and the fungi that connect them, along with certain chemicals they release into the air. Here again, the common usage of the word "brain" gets in the way of seeing different form-factors. There is no law that says all brains have to look alike.

Without an understanding of these basic principles, it's difficult to accept the reality of a universal mind, just as it took people a while to grasp electromagnetism in the late 1800s—how could something exert force and also be invisible? How could it have a structure—a field—and yet not have a physical form? There is another kind of "field," one similar to an electromagnetic field but of a different order—the field of mind. It is related to physical reality as we know it, but it is not restricted by it. Its inherent patterns of intelligence inform physical matter, from the subatomic level to the largest formations in the universe. Matter, one might say, is *mind made visible.*

All of this can be quite helpful in understanding the mechanics of mind, but it does not explain consciousness. Brain, mind, and intelligence describe the structure and activity of what most people call "consciousness," but these three elements are not consciousness itself; they are the mechanisms of consciousness. Just as mind is the organizing principle of matter, so is consciousness the organizing principle of mind. Mind is superior to matter; consciousness is superior to mind.

With all of our advancements in neuroscience and cognitive science, we are no closer to understanding the true nature of consciousness than our predecessors. We simply do not know what it is. There are, however, a few things we can say about it. While a plant "knows" which direction to point its leaves so as to get the most sunlight, it does so in a rather mechanistic way. It cannot, for instance, decide to do otherwise. That is not within its nature—plants can only do those things that promote their well-being. Human beings on the other hand...well, need I say more? We seem to have an infinite capacity for doing the dumbest things, even so far as to completely obliterate ourselves. It appears, at least in this regard, that plants are more intelligent than we are. But intelligence is not the same as consciousness.

In order to act against our own self-interest, there must be a part of us that is separate from the mind. The main theme of the movie, *Terminator 2, Judgment Day*, is "what makes a person a person?" One of the characters is a steel robot covered with a flesh and blood body. In terms of our working model here, he is *Nature*, a bio-mechanical machine programmed to act and react according to the demands of its own survival. The young boy symbolizes the Life Spirit, the "Christ child" nascent within humanity. He is the "hope of the nations," the possibility of self-transcendence, the driver of evolution for the human race. He is more interested in spiritual transformation than he is in form.

Consciousness is an ascendant force. It's only interested in growth and progression. Whereas Nature's tendency is to consolidate, consciousness continually seeks transformation. Nature, in this sense, is the alchemical element of Earth, and consciousness is Fire.

In mythic symbolism, such as we see in this movie, separate characters are often different aspects of one person. The boy in this case is our consciousness, that indefinable *something* that makes us divine beings. The robot is our physical body, which is a product of Nature. Its only concern is survival, and it will sacrifice consciousness whenever the interests of consciousness conflict with that goal. Nature is not interested in evolution; it's only interested in perpetuating itself in its present configuration. It can adapt to changing conditions, but it can only do so automatically. Consciousness, on the other hand, has the ability to adapt to an *ideal*. It continually seeks to align itself with that which has yet to be.

At the end of the movie, the robotic survival mentality must give way to the ascent of Spirit. But it's not an easy surrender. The robot is destroyed in a fiery cauldron of molten steel, the very image of transformation. But the robot cannot perform the sacrifice himself, because he can't go against his own programming, just as Nature cannot act against itself. Instead, he hands the controls to the boy, saying, "You do it. I cannot self-destruct."

Somewhere interwoven into the process of spiritual transformation is the act of self-sacrifice. "Unless you lose your life for my sake, you cannot find it." Couched within this saying of Jesus is a thread that can lead us out of the maze of materiality. Having the ability to reprogram ourselves, we are more than bio-mechanical machines. We are persons. We are spiritual.

More than anything else, the word "consciousness" refers to personhood. Being more than body, more than brain, and more than mind, a person has the power to self-destruct, which is another way of saying "self-transcend." We have the capability of destroying one form so that another form can take its place. All of the Christian iconography of death and resurrection symbolizes this principle. A "person" is not a derivative of form; a person is *above* form. Why? Because a person is made in the image and likeness of God, and God is *nameless* and *formless.*

It's the next step in this conceptual hierarchy of mind, intelligence, and consciousness that starts to push the limits of language in its ability to describe our reality. First, we have to forecast the possibility that there is something superior to consciousness, and we have to realize that whatever it is will not be within our ability to conceptualize. We will call it, for lack of a better term, *Being.* We have no way of describing it, because it is beyond description. Why? Because, in order to describe a thing, you must separate yourself from it. You must see it as an object—something apart from you. With Being, this is impossible. But while Being cannot be described or objectified, it can be *experienced.* Being is the foundation of all the world's esoteric and mystical teachings. Moses expressed it as "I am that I am." Jesus said, "I and the Father are one." He also said, "Before Abraham was, I am." Such statements only make sense when understood within the context of Being.

Human language focuses on nouns and verbs, things and actions. It is not set up to communicate Being. For instance, someone might say, "I am a man," not "I am *man-ing.*" To say that one is a "man" is to objectify a state of being, not speak it as an existential fact. This is another reason why Being cannot be described. It's why mystical statements like "I am that I am" are so inscrutable. The closest we've come to vocalizing a sense of it is the word "OM," or its westernized form, "amen." These words cause a vibratory condition in the head that silences thought, making it possible to clear one's consciousness of its contents. Since Being is immediately superior to consciousness, this uncluttered state of mind makes Being at the very least accessible—we can see it from there.

If we think that we are the interconnected thoughts and impressions that occupy our mind, that they comprise the totality of who we are, then we miss the boat entirely. We are not the mind; we are the Self. The Self is no-thing. By itself, it is devoid of content. It is the pure, undifferentiated field of potentiality, the vast inner space within the Being of God. Beyond words, beyond form, limitless—it is who we are in the most ultimate sense. The mind and its intelligence are used by the Self as a means to communicate in the world and, indeed, in all of the planes of existence given to us by God.

The Self does not move, not in the way our physical body moves through the material world. It just is. The mind is its field of activity, but it does not move through the mind; the mind moves around it the way the planets move around the Sun. All things within the mind are interconnected through it, the way the spokes of a wheel are all connected to each other by the wheel's hub. The Self moves by breathing in, drawing all things into itself, and then extends itself back out into creation by breathing out. But the Self does not move. It is the center that is everywhere, the immovable spot, the Holy of Holies, the *I AM*.

All of the Self's experiences are written upon its outermost sheath, the soul. Everything that happens to us, every action that we initiate, each interaction we have with others—all of this is recorded on our soul. Our soul is that small piece of the universal mind, the intelligence and coding specific to us, the patterns that govern the way we think and the way our physical body functions. It is the repository of all of the intelligence that makes us who we are as a unique individual. While the Self is the same in everyone, the soul is our energy signature, all of the characteristics we have acquired over the millennia of our existence. Along with the Self, the soul is *us*.

It's difficult to imagine a life where the center is all there is. It's like sitting in a movie theater getting lost in the stories unfolding on the screen. We sit in one place, but our mind is unfettered by space and time. This is how we experience the reality of our existence. The sights, the sounds, the feelings, the stories—they each leave their mark, and out of them we weave the tapestry of the being we call "I."

This is the essence of the expansive universal mind in which we live. Each occurrence is a nodal point in that mind, an intersection of subject and object, each indelibly imprinting itself on the other. There is no good or bad, just resonance and dissonance, compatibility and incompatibility, like and unlike. All of these are arranged in the symmetry they are capable of forming, governed by the perfect logic of the universal mind. Constantly coming into balance and going out of balance, and then coming into balance again, all in perfect, self-sustaining harmony and unfailing precision.

Each cycle of growth and development either strengthens or weakens our soul's overall pattern, its structure. The more focused we are, the stronger and healthier the structure gets. The more we are pulled around by external circumstances, the weaker and more fragmented it becomes. But the inherent nature of the soul is always towards integration. It is always seeking to right itself, to achieve inner harmony and symmetry, to align itself with the larger patterns in the mind of God. "Thy will be done, in Earth as it is in heaven."

The more it does this, the better able it is to act as a vehicle for the Self. But selfish acts and wrongful deeds only undermine the soul's noble intentions. The Roman poet, Ovid, said, "Ill habits gather by unseen degrees. As brooks make rivers, rivers run to seas." Habits of thought, habits of action, habits of affection, helpful or unhelpful—these are the energetic patterns that form the structure of our soul and through which the One Life expresses itself.

The Universal Mind of God is the milieu of the soul. It is a field of action unbounded by space and time. When Voltaire said, "God is a circle whose center is everywhere and circumference nowhere," his attempt was to jar the intellect out of its tendency to locate God within a framework the intellect can understand. By contemplating the relationships between mind, intelligence, consciousness, and Being, we improve our ability to function in the world of God.

CHAPTER 6

LOVE AND COMPASSION

The third element of religion's trilogy of universal truths is love and compassion. Compassion comes as a result of having experienced our oneness with the One Life. It is the state of consciousness that Jesus of Nazareth spoke *from* when he said, "Do unto others what you would have others do unto you." He didn't give this as a recipe but rather as a mode of being. He gave it as a means of realizing the truth of our oneness with each other, not as a way to get from point A to point B. Acting *as if* the Golden Rule were true causes the scales to drop from our eyes, and we begin to see the reality of what he was getting at. It's not something we have to attain; it's something we have to realize. It was here all along—we just didn't see it.

To get at this intellectually, ask yourself what would have to be true in order to make this oneness a reality?

Again, it's not like we're trying to get somewhere, but to see what already exists. As a means of approaching the truth, looking to see what already exists is as good a definition of faith as any. Faith is not taking an external idea and believing that it's true; faith is acting upon something that logic tells us *must* be true but is as yet unseen.

Here's an example of how to use this kind of faith as a means to realize your oneness with other people: Look at a wall, any wall, whether you're indoors or outdoors. Ask yourself, "What's on the other side of that wall?" You have never seen this particular wall, and you have no idea what's on the other side of it. But, only an insane person would think that nothing whatsoever exists beyond the wall, as though it were somehow the end of reality itself.

There's a science fiction story by Robert Heinlein, called *Orphans of the Sky*, where a spaceship is sent on a journey to a distant solar system in order to colonize one of its planets. The trip will take hundreds of years. The passengers will learn of their history and their mission as it is handed down from one generation to the next. But there's a rebellion, and all the historians are killed, thus destroying the community's links to both past and future. Since the spaceship has no windows, the people come to believe that the inside of the ship is all there is; they have no idea that they are on a vessel travelling through space. The bulkhead, the wall separating the inside of the ship from outer space, is simply the end of reality. They have no concept of something on the other side of it. They not only have no concept of it, they are incapable of entertaining such a thought! If you were to propose the possibility that there was something on the other side of the wall, they would think you were insane and simply ignore you.

What does this have to do with faith? Well, in this world, we know what walls are, at least the physical ones. We know that there is something beyond them, even if we can't see what it is. *This is faith.* We know something is there, because it *has to be.* Someone once said that if we did not know about the soul, we would have to invent it. Why? Because we would need some way to explain the invisible part of us that while unseen nevertheless produces visible effects in our lives.

Our oneness with each other is hidden from us by a wall, not a physical wall, but a real wall nonetheless. The wall between us is a conceptual one created by what our senses are capable of reporting—"I'm here, and you're over there; we are separate from one another." But, if you've ever had an experience that even remotely resembles telepathy or synchronicity, you know that there are invisible lines of communication connecting us to each other, lines that enable us to know and feel what someone else is thinking and feeling, even at great distances.

There is another aspect to our oneness with each other that more than anything else makes love and compassion possible. It's the saying, "There but for the grace of God go I." The human condition varies widely from person to person. One person is rich, while others are poor; one is healthy, while others are sick; one is in a relationship, while others are lonely. But we know that the dividing line between ourselves and others who are less fortunate is a thin one indeed. When we sense our own frailty, we are more apt to feel compassion for others.

But here's the one thing that helps us understand compassion the most. If oneness is a reality (and we know that it is) then the thoughts that float through our heads are not necessarily our own. In fact, they are probably not. It is far more likely that we don't think at all but merely re-think pre-existing thoughts, thoughts that have been circulating in the shared mind of humanity for centuries.

When we relate to each other as if we were one, it gets harder to take what others say as a personal attack upon ourselves, because they do not necessarily know what they are thinking. They probably think they do, but chances are they are merely repeating ideas that have become permanent fixtures of the human mind. These might even be literal fixtures, because as the human brain evolves, oft-repeated thoughts become part of its neural architecture, and these changes are passed down genetically from one generation to the next. The creation recreates the creator.

If this is true about the human mind and brain, then the mere suggestion of a word will trigger an entire file of associated narratives. This is called "framing," and it is so much a part of how we think that we can hardly think any other way. But love and compassion short-circuit this process. When we shut off our thoughts and love someone, the *wall of words* separating us starts to disappear.

Words separate us, but love unites us. This sounds trite, but it's true. And the more we love other people, the more we can see ourselves in them. We do the same things they do, which is why their actions can annoy us so much—they remind us of ourselves! This is why religions place love and compassion at the top of their lists.

In the movie *Ender's Game*, Ben Kingsley's character says, "The more you understand your enemy, the more you love him." When we come to see the automatic nature of the human mind and how most of our thoughts come pre-packaged, handed down to us not just culturally but in the actual neural pathways of our brain, then we see that most people are asleep. The things they say and do are mostly unintentional; they have nothing to do with who they really are. "Forgive them Father, for they know not what they do." Knowing this makes love and compassion possible.

The Priesthood comes from the Self, not from the mind. If it came from the mind, then it would be flawed, because the human mind has all sorts of thoughts that it has accumulated over the millennia that are fundamentally anti-social. If we base our Priesthood on ideas and concepts—points of Scripture and doctrine—then we cannot avoid hating each other, because the ideas and concepts themselves are devised to emphasize differences, not commonalities. They are the result of all of humanity's history condensed into thought-forms and neural patterns dedicated exclusively to the survival of tribal identity.

So, if thinking is the problem, it stands to reason that NOT thinking might be a way out. Can we interact with life and other people and not think? Can we let go of our need to assess, judge, evaluate, and discriminate and just simply BE with the other person? Unless we can do this, we cannot be loving and compassionate, and we certainly cannot be functioning priests.

Nothing brings people closer together than a shared hardship. And if the human condition as I have described it here isn't a shared hardship, I don't know what is. The only thing worse than thinking your thoughts are your own is... well, thinking that your thoughts are your own. There is nothing worse. Granted, it's not that original thought is impossible, it's that it is exceedingly rare. Knowing this makes it a lot easier to cut yourself and others a whole lot of slack, and maybe have a good laugh in the process!

PART 2

WHAT PRIESTS DO

CHAPTER 7

OWNING THE
COLLECTIVE MIND

If we are honest with ourselves, we know that our thoughts are not our own. Our minds are like a person walking down a street of musicians, each one playing a different tune, and our body involuntarily dances to each one of them as we pass by. This is the way our minds work most of the time—no composure, no self-control. The slightest suggestion of an idea—*any idea*—sends us off on a tangent. We have completely relinquished control of our thinking and given it to the world. The world around us is the cause, and we are the effect.

In terms of stimulus and response, we are like an amoeba, responding only to changes in our environment without any real direction of our own. Advertisers are especially adept at hiding ideas within ideas, getting us to accept underlying premises without consciously knowing what they are. This condition is a little better than the amoeba's, but we are still at the effect of external causes, even if we carry those causes inside our own heads.

The real question is this: how do we become a cause in the world? In other words, how do we become a *priest*? If we rely upon our own ideas—right and wrong, beautiful and ugly, moral and immoral, just and unjust, sacred and profane—and we superimpose these ideas onto the collective mind of the crowd, we are not really being a cause. Rather, we are being a *replicator*—a replicator of pre-existing thoughts.

So, what are we to do? How do we function as a priest? How do we act instead of react? How do we become a causal agent in the world? As long as we have preconceptions about right and wrong, we cannot avoid making mistakes, because we never know for sure what's really needed in any given situation.

The answer to this question is a paradox: we do the right thing by doing nothing. That's right, *nothing*. We neither act nor react. When we remove the "this is right" and "that is wrong" from our mental atmosphere, we begin to wake up from the mesmerizing effects of our own preconceptions. The filters we have so carefully constructed over a lifetime start to drop away. For the first time, perhaps, we see the world as it is and not how we expect it to be. Our minds become pure, free of bias, a clearing in a dense jungle. And that clearing sets up a potential (speaking in terms of energy) that causes action to happen without itself becoming part of the action. Our very presence becomes a catalyst. And the ability to act as a catalyst is one of the primary prerequisites of the Priesthood.

If we can rid ourselves of judgment and simply be in the moment, being neither drawn to nor repelled by what we see around us, then we become the eye of the storm, the clear space around which the swirl will organize itself. As long as we remain the eye of the storm, the swirl will not touch us. But, if we lose our center and begin to identify with the swirl, we will get caught in its updraft. The stronger the storm system, the more violently will it suck us into the situation. *"If your eye is filled with darkness, how great will be that darkness!"* This applies to our inner storms as well as the ones we encounter in the world.

It's not easy remaining calm in a storm. It takes many years of practice and a certain resignation to the impermanence of life. But, even more than that, it takes a steadfast resolve to do what's right at any cost. Doing the right thing builds strength, especially when the cost is high.

Too often we judge the rightness and wrongness of a situation by taking sides. We rush in to defend the victim and condemn the perpetrator. Rarely do we see the big picture, the cause behind the effect, the history leading up to the injustice. Rather, we let the sound bite on the morning news shape our thinking. Such an assessment almost always has us chasing the story rather than cutting through the spin and hyperbole to discern the roots of the problem.

As priests, our proper sphere of action is in the realm of cause, and our job as teachers is to reveal the realm of cause in the minds of our students. Unfortunately, many priests prefer to preach against bad behavior than to teach proper thinking. It does no good to say murder is wrong—we all know that. What we need to learn is how to control our emotional reactions. We need to understand the cycle of violence and not pretend that it doesn't exist. We need to learn the cause and effect relationship between our thoughts and our feelings—that violent thoughts lead to violent actions.

When a movie's chief purpose is to arouse the instinct for revenge, teaching that injustices are best settled with violence, priests need to speak up. Such movies are little more than emotional porn. They reinforce black-and-white thinking by drawing sharp lines of contrast between the good guys and the villains. With this, the movie producers offer a quick and intellectually cheap solution to life's complex problems, which sells lots of tickets but does little to edify one's moral sensibilities. A steady diet of this makes us easily controlled by military and political interests. When Hollywood panders to the desire to demonize one's enemies, thus making them easier to kill, it is a priest's duty to point out the obvious. We are, after all, the *good* shepherds. We should act like it and put the wolves in their place.

It's hard to think clearly when we are upset. If you want people to do your bidding, you must first make sure that they are upset most of the time, so that they are unable to think. Thinking people are harder to rule than those who are simply looking for ways to relieve their frustrations. For them, you simply create a problem and then present the solution. The first thing priests teach their students, therefore, is how to take careful inventory of their thoughts as they occur and not blindly accept whatever goes through their minds. Once people can observe their own thinking and understand that their thoughts are not necessarily their own, they can then learn how to modify them in ways that mitigate emotional reactions. This is the first step in giving people the means by which they can start taking control of their lives.

Taking ownership of the collective mind of humanity sounds preposterous, does it not? Let me explain what I mean by "owning" the collective mind. Once we learn that the mind is a universal medium into which we all plug ourselves, we then learn that most thoughts that occur to us do not originate in our own brain. As we talked about before, most thoughts are pre-existing entities in the greater mind. We merely rethink them when the conditions are right. Our reactions are like train tracks that have already been laid; we have no choice but to go down them whenever we start moving in their general direction. So, taking ownership of the collective mind is to start thinking in terms of *laying new tracks.* How do we do that?

Here are some basic principles to consider. Deliberate thinking is more powerful than reactive thinking. Deliberate thinking is when we first decide what to think and then think it. When we contemplate the cause and effect relationships between ideas and actions (and not merely go along for the ride whenever we are presented with an issue) we begin to see that it matters—*a lot*—how we think about a problem. Notice that I said *how* we think, not *what* we think. What we think is nothing more than opinion; it's how we think that has the power to make a difference in the collective mind.

If we think, for example, that income inequality is wrong and that those who orchestrate it should be punished, then we are having an opinion. Those whom we are calling "perpetrators" have their opinions about the matter as well, which they believe are just as valid as our own. No matter how much we place the emphasis on our opinion, they are able to match it. In fact, the rules of that game demand that they do. Winning is everything in the realm of opinion. No opinion, regardless of how well-reasoned it is, has the power to prevail against other opinions. Opinions are powerless.

The thing that *does* give our thoughts power is our *knowing.*

Knowing is a much misunderstood word. When Jesus said, "You shall know the truth, and the truth shall set you free," he wasn't talking about a set of ideas. He wasn't saying that if you know all the verses in the Bible that you will suddenly and miraculously acquire complete control of your destiny. The emphasis in his statement was not on the word "truth" but on the word "know." How do we know where he placed his emphasis? Because the word "truth" implies a set of ideas, whereas the word "know" indicates action. Ideas are powerless until they are put into action.

Knowing is the conviction that your thoughts will prevail. It is understanding that thought has power, that in the world of cause and effect, thought *IS* cause. It's not that you believe that you're right, it's that you know that your thought *must* manifest, because that's how the creative medium of mind works. When the centurion told Jesus that all Jesus had to do was speak the Word and the centurion's servant would be healed, he understood that God, the great Creative Intelligence of the Universe, *had* to respond. He understood the true nature of authority.

It doesn't matter if a thought is good or evil; the Law of Mind is completely impersonal in this regard. History has proven over and over again that powerful ideas don't necessarily have to be moral ideas. Alexander the Great said that if a man can keep his mind focused on one idea for just three minutes, he is capable of conquering the world. Every person who has ever accomplished anything of significance knows this principle. Keep your eye on the ball and you will reach your goal every time. Know what you want, never give up, follow your dream—the clichés are endless, but true. The difference, however, between a priest and a merely successful person is that a priest has taken a vow of Service and knows how to maximize the Law of Mind for the good of all. A priest knows that when his or her Word is aligned with the will of God, nothing can stand in its way. And it is this knowing that gives the Priesthood its authority in the life of the world.

Priests do, however, have the ability to assert their own will, even when it's contrary to God's will, but their results will always fail eventually, because independent creations cannot exist forever in the greater system. In order to live, they must be in accord with the overall scheme of things. An idea can be a good idea but still be out of accord with God's will if it is asserted at the wrong time. But an idea whose time has come and is backed by the knowing of a functioning priest—a priest who understands the laws of creation and how to use them—that idea is unstoppable. It *will* manifest.

This isn't magic; it's the way creation actually works. We can change conditions if we understand the forces that are already in action and then steer them to an alternative outcome. For example, lightning can be redirected through a lightning rod. We can even put it to constructive use by connecting the lightning rod to a cistern to purify the water. We haven't violated the Law of Cause and Effect; *we have simply steered it to produce a different outcome.*

Here's an analogy: a sentence has two principal elements—a noun (subject) and a verb (action). Once written, the story is complete. It's a closed circuit, just like the circle with a dot in the center. But add a modifier and the energy inherent in the story can be *steered*. You're not changing the elements, but you are *directing* them. The modifier is the third element. It is what makes it possible to *adapt* the energy of the narrative to the outcome we want.

> *It is true without untruth, certain and most true, that which is below is like that which is on high, and that which is on high is like that which is below; by these things are made the miracles of one thing. And as all things are, and come from One, by the mediation of One, so all things are born from this unique thing by* **adaptation**. – Hermes

Being morally right does not make us effective priests; knowing the laws of creation and how to use the Word does. When the centurion told Jesus that all he had to do was say the word and his servant would be healed, he demonstrated that he understood the true nature of a command. He didn't say, "Ask the Father to heal my servant"; he said, "Command that this be done." This is the line of demarcation between a priest and the rest of humanity. It is the ability to command the forces within the One Mind.

Here's how we do that. When we enter the Priesthood, we leave the world. This is necessary, because spiritual power cannot be exercised at the same level as the effects it is intended to produce. This is the principle that Albert Einstein was getting at when he said, "The significant problems we face cannot be solved at the same level of thinking we were at when we created them." He also said, "A problem never exists in isolation; it is surrounded by other problems in space and time. The more of the context of a problem that a scientist [*or priest*] can comprehend, the greater are his chances of finding a truly adequate solution." The only adequate solution is to change the *cause* of the problem, not merely fix its effects. Priests operate in the domain of cause.

A command—the *Word*—is not yelling at the effects. It is *calling forth* the reality that lies behind them. To illustrate, let's look at another example, this time from the Gospel of John—the raising of Lazarus from the dead. Jesus didn't say, "Lazarus, don't be dead!" Nor did he say, "Lazarus, be alive!" What he said was, "Lazarus, *come forth!*" If he had said, "Be alive," the implication would have been that he was currently dead. But Jesus looked beyond the appearance to the reality—*there is no death*— and then commanded Lazarus to take action. Jesus raised his consciousness to a higher *context*, to that level of reality behind the world of appearances.

The story of Lazarus is worth looking at in detail. As with most stories in the Bible, it contains a deeper meaning than what we find when we take it literally. Let's break the action down into its crucial elements. The story of the resurrection of Lazarus starts off by setting up the scene.

First, Jesus hears of Lazarus' death and decides to go to his home, despite warnings that local officials are trying to arrest him. Next, when he gets there, he comfort's Lazarus' sisters. Not only that, he tells them that he is going to resurrect Lazarus. Other details are filled in—the fact that Jesus loved Lazarus and is moved to tears by his passing, the fact that Lazarus has been in the grave for four days and that his body is in a state of decomposition, and the family's bewilderment at Jesus' late arrival when they know that Lazarus was his beloved friend. But, all of this is only the backdrop for what happens next, the *real* action of the story.

Jesus does three things. (Always pay close attention when the Bible divides stories into three parts!) First, he tells the others to remove the stone from the mouth of the burial cave. Next, he commands Lazarus to *come forth!* Then, he directs them to remove his burial cloths and to let him go. These are three distinct components of the action of raising Lazarus from the dead. Let's examine them individually:

Oh, wait...there are really four things. But the fourth thing, which comes before the other three, is really the prelude to the action, not the action itself. It's where Jesus says, "Father, I thank thee that thou hast heard me. And I knew that thou hearest me always: but because of the people which stand by I said it, that they may believe that thou hast sent me." This is Jesus setting the context within which the action will take place—the Infinite Creative Intelligence of the Universe, God. It's an absolutely necessary part of the action, but it's the platform from which the action springs forth, not the action itself. It is *knowing*.

1. Jesus prepares the field of action by ordering that the stone blocking the entrance of the cave be removed. He doesn't remove it himself but rather orders that it be done. This is where we command the forces of nature to go where we want them to go, as in the example above where we redirect the lightning by placing a metal rod on top of the house and connecting it to ground. This shows that using the Word requires real action in the world, that we prepare the way for manifestation to take place.

2. Jesus commands Lazarus to come out of the tomb. This is the actual result Jesus is looking for, the thing he wants to accomplish. This is where he *speaks* the Word directly into the reality underlying the appearance, ordering it to reveal itself. He speaks this with *executive authority*, which is the key to speaking the Word. He speaks it from the center of his being with the absolute knowing that it will be fulfilled—*"Father, I thank thee that thou hast heard me."* He doesn't ask; he *commands*.

3. Jesus reintegrates Lazarus back into the world, declaring his freedom to live his life. This shows that once a creation is set in motion, we have to let it go. This is exactly what God did when the world was created. The Divine had to release it so that it could find the full extent of its own self-expression, not knowing how it would all play out. This factor of *unknowability* is what sets creation apart from mere replication. It's what makes the Breath of Life *alive*. Unless a thing is free to choose its own path, it's not really alive. And this is what we have to

include whenever we call something forth from the field of pure potential.

Every time we envision a new product, a new business plan, an idea for a novel, the floor plan for a new house, a new pharmaceutical drug, or an alternative energy source, we are calling it forth from the field of pure potential. This is how creation works. It is *real!*

So, this is what priests do—we speak the Word. We call forth the reality of God from its hiding place in the tomb of matter. In the Gospel of Thomas, Jesus says, "The kingdom of heaven is spread upon the Earth, but men do not see it." Our job as priests is to unconceal that which is already here, the reality of God that is hiding just behind the veil of matter. Unless we do this, none of the rest will make much difference in the spiritual evolution of humanity. We are the midwives, the agents of change, the shepherds of souls—and all of this by the grace of God and the help of those above.

CHAPTER 8

THE MYSTIC PRIEST

The Mysteries are those things of God that are beyond the capability of the human mind to understand—they cannot be apprehended intellectually. The very instant we think we have them figured out, they elude us, and we slide back into the mind, that hall of mirrors that reflects itself back onto itself *ad infinitum*. We have to look deeper. Always. The word "mystery" implies this—it's an *invitation*, not a prohibition. But, while the Mysteries cannot be intellectually apprehended, they can be experienced through direct perception. If the intellect is the mind's computer, direct experience is the person *using* the computer. We are more than our intellect.

There are few words in modern day English that have been as discredited as the words *mystery, mystic,* and *irrational*. There is a deep distrust in modern society of the "irrational" mind. This is largely due to Sigmund Freud's belief that mankind is nothing more than a bunch of murderous thugs held in check by the thinnest veneer of social conditioning. Add to that Ayn Rand's deification of the rational mind (and her belief that mysticism is knowledge *without effort*) and you get a subconscious filled with chaos and confusion, a Pandora's Box that must be kept locked at all times. This is why some religious folks regard meditation as reckless and dangerous, opening one up to demon possession (limbic forces), because to probe the subconscious, they believe, is to invite disaster. But for mystic priests, the subconscious mind is their regular beat. They work the night shift, carrying out their duties in prayer, blessing, and soul healing. And they do it in the same way that the Mysteries work upon us, by planting seeds deep within us and then patiently waiting for them to sprout.

The work of the mystic priest differs from that of an occultist in one significant way: the primary actor in any action is God. Just as the Mysteries act upon us by grace, which is to say by God and not by our own efforts, mystic priests work in a state of not-knowing. They look at a situation or person and say, "I *do not know* what is needed here." The occultist, on the other hand, seeks to overlay the problem with a template constructed from his or her own understanding. Mystic priests leave that up to God. They realize that the intelligence of the Divine Mind is far superior to their own. They act as midwife, not designer. By saying "I don't know," mystic priests create the opening through which God can work. And, they know to *keep their hands off of the process.*

Mystic priests approach a problem with an eye to its potential solution, knowing that a solution exists but not knowing what it is. Just as the Mysteries present us with a mental image of a divine truth without intellectually describing it, so do mystic priests hold a problem up to God as though it were a chalice held above the altar, with the full expectation that it will be transformed into perfection. Our problems, in a sense, are *God's* mysteries, and God does love to solve them!

Humility is the hallmark of the mystic priest. Humility is the attitude, the frame of mind that allows the priest to get out of the way and to let the process of transformation do its work. That process is simply more than the human mind can comprehend. Pride, on the other hand, is the attitude or frame of mind that wants to sit in the director's chair, to feel the power, and to take the credit. It sees itself as the broker of the action, wanting to orchestrate its every move. And because the human mind is limited, it can only restrict the process of transformation—a heavy price to pay for a little ego aggrandizement.

Pride keeps the Mysteries from acting upon us. When we think that we already know God, then what began as an immediate experience turns into a static memory, and we wind up worshiping an idol of the mind. But devotion fosters trust, and trust is necessary if we are to willingly open ourselves up to the unknown. This, of course, takes humility, which is itself a great source of power and transformation.

CHAPTER 9

DEVOTION

There are two powerful forces in our lives—desire and fear. We are born with them. It is as though we are an electrically charged particle either attracted to or repelled from the ever-changing circumstances of our lives. Rarely, except in brief moments of clarity, do we experience peace—deep, soul-satisfying *peace*. And for those of us on the spiritual path, this predicament can be hell.

In fact, every move we make towards God seems to precipitate an encounter with the devil. Like Luke Skywalker in his training with Yoda, in order to become a Jedi warrior, we must first face our deepest fears. As you may recall, Luke had to enter the cave of initiation where he had to face his unknown terror. In order to pass the test, however, he had to do so without reacting. From deep within the cavern, Darth Vader emerged with his sword drawn. Luke was overcome with fear and struck out at the phantasm and thus failed the test. His fears, like ours, can seem *so* real.

Our desires can undo us just as thoroughly as our fears. When I was a young boy, periodically I would be overcome with an intense longing to connect. My heart seemed to swell out of my body, surrounding me with an aching desire for something I could neither see nor name. All of the beauty in the world would arch itself skyward, pulling me (without instructing me) towards some promise, some prize of fulfillment, some homecoming that I could not identify. The feeling was both joyful and excruciating. Of course, my ten or eleven year-old brain could only interpret this as wanting a girlfriend, even though no human person could ever fill such a gaping hole. It was as though my internal magnet had suddenly been dialed all the way up, so high that nothing on Earth could satisfy its longing. More often than not, this unfulfilled desire would leave me feeling depressed and alone.

This feeling eventually became internalized (read: *buried*) and I began that eternal pursuit for happiness in the world. But it was like looking for an oasis in a desert. My desire led me to extremes in all areas of my life, as though I were trying to crack the world open with the sheer force of my longing, thinking that somewhere within it I would find gold. Fortunately, I found a spiritual teacher, and with the adept hand of an accomplished master, he led me out of the desert and into my heart. He gave me a way to channel my longing, to redirect my searching away from the Earth and into the stratosphere of spiritual attainment. The heavens opened up, and I finally found what I was seeking. What once had seemed like a chasm of unfulfillment now spread itself out before me like a vast, overhead vault of stellar brilliance. He brought me into the light and into direct contact with the face of God.

Along with this huge infusion of cash into my spiritual bank account came all the problems that lottery winners encounter when their lives are suddenly upended by good fortune. Many of these people wind up destitute, because they cannot adjust to the increased energy. Their normal inability to manage money gets magnified exponentially, and all of their bad habits come out in force like unwanted relatives demanding their piece of the pie. The exact same thing happens when spiritual awakening suddenly expands our consciousness. Everything left unattended makes itself known with a vengeance. Even when one's training involves combing out most of the inner tangles, as mine did, a whole new layer of convoluted problems gets exposed. What normally would have taken decades to emerge into my consciousness suddenly surfaced like a whale at speed, spouting fury and creating mayhem on the surface of my self-awareness. Awakening, as it turns out, comes with a price.

Why does this happen? Spiritual work—the expansion of consciousness into divine realms—is like taking the resistance out of an electrical circuit. When you lower resistance, you increase the current. When the current is increased, everything is "amped up"—more heat, more light, and more energy for all of the surprises which up until now have been safely locked away in Pandora's Box. In short, *all hell breaks loose!* Spiritual teachers throughout the millennia have asked themselves, "Do I tell him what he's in for, or not?" They default in the timeworn way—they turn the experience into a story, pit a young hero against insurmountable odds, make him go through trials and tribulations, even *death*, and then resurrect him in glorious victory. Sound familiar?

With every awakening comes a trial—every spiritual advancement necessitates a campaign to clean up what floats to the surface. Immediately following Jesus' baptism, he is led into the wilderness to confront his demons. Similarly, after his glorious encounter with the great ones of old on the Mount of Transfiguration, he is led into Jerusalem and to Golgotha. When the light within us is turned up, all of our shadows intensify. This is the blessing and the curse of spiritual awakening. It is why Jesus said, "For which of you, intending to build a tower, sitteth not down first, and counteth the cost, whether he have sufficient to finish it?" This is similar to what the 19th Century Indian mystic, Ramakrishna, said: "Do not seek illumination unless you seek it as a man whose hair is on fire seeks a pond." Anything short of this will not provide the necessary heat you will need to turn your psychic lead into gold.

Here's the kicker, the one thing that has proved the undoing of many a spiritual aspirant: You cannot talk your way out of this dilemma. No amount of intellectualization will defuse the demons that rear up as a result of you being energized by spiritual awakening. It doesn't matter how many books you read or how many seminars you attend, there are no substitutes for the pick-and-shovel work you are going to have to do to clean this up. What you are dealing with is deeply ontological, and it is at this level that you are going to have to engage.

Fortunately, there's a way out. It is clearly spelled out in the story of Jesus' temptations in the wilderness—"clearly" if you know how to read it. First, you have to recognize that there is no external devil tempting Jesus. This is strictly an inside job. The temptations arise from *within* Jesus himself. These are his own unresolved issues that he has to deal with before he can embark on his mission as teacher and messiah. And before you say that Jesus didn't have any issues, that he was perfect, consider this: if he didn't have unresolved issues, he would not have been able to overcome them, and we would not have a "Way" to resolve them in ourselves. This is the sacrifice made by the Christ Being when It came to Earth in a physical body—to undergo the human experience in order to raise it up to its divine potential. If he had been "perfect" from the outset, the Way would have been unattainable to us.

The temptations, three in number, are roughly this—satisfying physical appetites, succumbing to fear, and becoming arrogant. Turn these stones into bread; throw yourself off of this cliff; use your powers to rule the world. The exact same issues came up for Siddhartha at the time of his enlightenment—the sexual advances of Mara's daughters; a barrage of arrows flying at his head; the feelings of obligation to rule as his father's heir to the throne. Understanding this precedent in the life of the Buddha helps us to understand the Three Temptations of Christ.

The important element in both of these accounts is this— neither Buddha nor Jesus resorted to intellectualization to solve their problems. They didn't try to talk their way out of the situation. Instead, they appealed to a higher power. In all three stages of Jesus' process, rather than argue with the devil, he quotes Scripture. He doesn't give his *reasons* why he won't give in. Instead, he lifts his consciousness to God. It was as though he connected one end of a wire to his inner conflicts and the other end to heaven, like a lightning rod. He equalized the potential through the medium of his own consciousness. Buddha did the same when he "touched the Earth." This is how we do it. We don't grapple with our problems. We lift them up to God.

When we find ourselves in the grip of our desires and our fears, it is our devotion that saves us. It is the power of the heart, not the mind, that grounds us in heaven. We need only to look up, to change the direction of our attention, taking it off of the situation and placing it on that which is higher. How? Through prayer and meditation. This is the workshop of spiritual awakening. We go within. We take each issue as it arises, whether of fear or desire, and lift it up as we would a chalice at the altar. We lift it up and connect it to God's consciousness, the infinite creative power of the Universe. We lift it up with the same intensity of feeling that a small child has when she strains to reach the cookie jar on the kitchen counter. That's how badly we want it! We reach with our heart, not with our mind. This is devotion.

Luckily, we're not always struggling with our fears and desires. But this shouldn't keep us from reaching up to God with our heart on a regular basis. We stay in shape. We don't wait until the morning of the race to work out. We train every day so that when a crisis comes, we're prepared. Too often, we wait until we're in the soup before we turn to God, and then we wonder why it's so hard to rise above our problems. We need to make it a consistent practice, not just a port in a storm. We turn our relationship with God into a love affair—God as *lover*, not as sugar daddy.

It is through our devotion to God that we are "saved," not the strength of our mind. The brain is fragile; the heart is an indomitable muscle. It's easy to be loyal when you're in love. Connect with God—*be in love!*

CHAPTER 10

THE ENERGY OF RITUAL

When we meditate, we "go within." We withdraw our attention from the world and pull it back into ourselves— we turn away from the world *out there.* It is something that martial artists, dancers, and athletes of all kinds experience regularly. It is what we are doing energetically when we fold our hands in front of us in prayer. We take the energy that is normally squandered on outer distractions and focus it inwardly, drawing it back into ourselves, forming a tight cocoon of light and power.

As we become more and more successful at this, we acquire the ability to turn away from the external world altogether during our meditations. We are able to become oblivious to what's going on around us. Our consciousness becomes a laboratory wherein we can work and pray, which is what "laboratory" means (labor + oratory). In effect, we are withdrawing our attention from the world and gathering it into a singular, inner focal point.

For the ordinary person, withdrawing energy from the world and focusing it within has the sole purpose of transforming one's consciousness. We take something that is ordinarily diffused and we concentrate it into a small space. As we concentrate it, it becomes more potent. If we keep it within ourselves, that potency works on us and changes us, just as fire changes whatever it contacts. But as priests, we take this potential and direct it outwards into an image we have formed in mind.

The image is set up on the altar of our imagination. It is directly in front of us. And since we have mastered the ability to separate our attention from the outer world of our senses and focus it entirely on the inner field of our awareness, the image before us exists solely in mind with no interference from external vibrations. We are operating under a cloak, so to speak, in a kind of spiritual "clean room."

What I am describing here is the work of an *occultist*. Normally, such work is only carried out by those who have been carefully trained to do it. Otherwise, these actions are performed through the format of established rituals, such as the sacraments of Communion and Baptism. But unless we learn to perform simple energy work such as this, we cannot really perform the sacraments effectively. Therefore, we have to experiment. We have to become totally familiar with how energy works and what it can accomplish, first by learning how to draw it in and then project it out.

Attention is a funny thing. It is only as good as it is grounded. What do I mean by this? When our attention is pulled all over the place, dictated as it were by outer circumstances, we have little control over where it goes. When we are in that position, we cannot use the Law of Mind to create what we want to create, but only re-create what is already going on. In order to use the Law effectively and create something *new*, we have to be able to ignore outer circumstances and visualize only what we want. And, we have to *embody* the thing we are trying to create.

What does it mean to embody a thing? In spiritual work, you cannot get from point A to point B by *going* somewhere. A gets to B by *becoming* B. Unless we embody the essential characteristics of the thing we are trying to create, we cannot bring it into manifestation. This is why, for example, we "take on" the Lord Jesus Christ when we say Communion. Unless we become him, we cannot say with any effect, "This is my body."

Priests practice inner alchemy, and the altar is their workbench. Every element on the altar—the paten, the chalice, the eternal flame, the candles, the wine and bread—both symbolize and embody sacred principles. After all, Christianity is the religion of *incarnation*. Unless we touch the Earth, as Buddha did when he came into enlightenment, and as Jesus did when the blood of his crucifixion entered the ground, nothing changes. Buddha was the awakening of humanity, Christ was its salvation—right thinking and right action, purified mind and purified heart.

The altar itself symbolizes the heart. It is there that we make our sacrifices. The word "sacrifice" has an alchemical meaning. It means taking one thing and transmuting it into another. In animal sacrifice, the rising smoke of the burnt offering was thought to ascend to heaven, bringing with it the prayers of those making the offering. The body of the animal became a vehicle of communication with the Divine. Later, Jesus would embody this form of sacrifice, making his own vehicle, his body and blood, the sacrificial offering, and thus a channel for grace. When he said that we must follow him, he meant that we too must offer *our* vehicles, our body and blood, as vehicles for God›s grace to enter the world. But ours is a *living* sacrifice, not a literal death.

As priests, we find our altar within ourselves, and we take one form of energy and transform it into another. We do this, not by our own power, but by raising it up to God, just as we raise the elements of wine and bread. The act of physically raising the chalice and paten above the altar symbolizes raising the vibration of the matter of which the elements are composed. We lift them up so that they are "closer to heaven," the divine fire that changes everything it touches. The old word for this was "quickening." Today, we understand it as increasing its rate of vibration.

In order to understand this process, one only needs to find that place within where lower passions are transmuted into noble purpose—anger into resolve, lust into love, greed into generosity. Once that place is identified, we observe the action itself. This is what we play out at the altar. We engage the body, the mind, and the heart in an action that directly corresponds to what we are doing inwardly, which is forming a connection with God and letting the grace pour into us. The physical elements of the wine and bread cannot help but be affected. If we unify the inner with the outer, they will be literally transformed. Their vibrational quality will be changed.

Just as some people have developed the ability to pick up the vibrations of other people from the objects they have touched, so do the recipients of the transformed elements of the Eucharist pick up the vibrations of the ascended Christ Jesus. Through the mind and body of the priest—her intention, her will, and her spoken Word—the Christ infuses itself into the wine and bread, causing it to resonate with the Christ's own blood and body, which now exist above the vibrational plane of the material world.

When priests perform the mass with this understanding, and when they have developed their spiritual consciousness to where they can sense the heaven worlds, then this transmutation can take place. It is an energetic event, spanning two worlds, two dimensions, one that can be felt by everyone who participates in it. No amount of explanation, however, can convey the reality of this. Only by practicing it can the reality of the transmutation become part of the reality of the priest and the recipients.

The secret of alchemy is that the transmutation takes place within *you*, not within the external elements, except as they take on the vibration of the heaven world that you contact. The wine and bread become the vehicles for the vibrational quality of the Christ, just as your body and blood become the vehicle for God's grace. Heaven and Earth occupy different strata in the world of God. Priests, by the use of ritual and their own developed spiritual consciousness, are the bridge between these two realities. This is what makes the sacrament of Communion *sacred*.

There is a saying: "Where attention goes, energy flows." Taken at face value, it means that we give life to whatever we think about. Simple enough, right? Every marketing person knows that the first thing you have to do to make a sale is *get their attention*. What they don't know is that as consciousness moves from one object to another, there is a corresponding movement of energy.

Every movement at the altar is choreographed to produce certain effects. Why is the bread on the left and the wine on the right? Why is the Body served first and then the Blood? Not only does position matter, but *sequence* matters as well. And I don't mean that it matters semantically or because it was scripted that way. It matters because if you change the position or the sequence, *you change the energy*.

The human body, *our* body, along with being called our "vehicle," is also sometimes referred to as our *"instrument."* We use our body on this plane of manifestation the same way a trades person uses his or her tools to effect changes in their materials. We *use* our body the way they use their tools. What we *construct* are patterns of energy. We construct these patterns by the way we move, the way we think, and the words we speak. The more integrity our construction has—the more consistent we are in building the pattern—the more power will move through it. This is why we perform the Mass the same way every time. Not that we can't allow room for the Spirit to express Itself in new ways occasionally, but the basic structure remains the same. The more we use it, the stronger it gets. And, as more people use it, especially at cardinal times of the year, it gets stronger still.

As with most things of an esoteric nature, explanations are never sufficient to get the point across. You have to experience it. So, here's something you can try. The next time you are about to raise the chalice to do the transmutation, pause for a moment and look at it while it is sitting there on the altar. Think to yourself, "This is wine." Then, as you raise it high above your head, and you reach up in consciousness to the Christ Being of the Sun (which is *everywhere*), and you feel its energy surround and infuse the cup, look again. What has changed? The wine you raised up is not the wine you set back down.

Now, imagine doing that in reverse. Not with the wine, of course, but with anything, with your *consciousness*. What happens when you look up and contact the Christ Being first, and then *bring it down* into something here on the Earth plane? Here we have both a difference in direction and in sequence. Therefore, we will have a difference in the energy and the form in which it manifests. "Verily I say unto you, Whatsoever ye shall bind on earth shall be bound in heaven: and whatsoever ye shall loose on earth shall be loosed in heaven." What we look upon while in Christ consciousness, we add power to it—the power to solidify or substantiate. But when we first look upon something and *then* take it to Christ consciousness, we release it from the Earth. These are basic alchemical principles.

We do this all the time. Whenever we look at anything with the intention of understanding its true nature, we bring Spirit to bear upon it. We isolate it in the mind and cause it to reveal itself *as it is*. But when we look upon a thing in order to see its potential, we remove the restrictions imposed upon it by the forces of Earth and unconceal what it might become.

These are the fundamental aspects of ritual—raising up and bringing down. The physical actions are, of course, symbolic. But, they also set a pattern, just like the wires in a house or nerves in the body. The intention with which you perform the action is the real part, combined with your knowing that your actions are causes that *must* create effects (faith). Everything begins in mind; change something there and it must show up here. But, you must first know that you can.

In neuro-linguistic programming (NLP), we learn the importance of bodily gestures, eye movements, and vocal intonations, and the way these things affect consciousness and behavior. This is not new knowledge. Nor is it only based on the way the brain works. The brain works the way it does because it is a reflection of the Cosmos. Those who instituted the Priesthood and the Sacraments knew the reality of *As Above, So Below*, and they could read the "stars" both in the heavens and in the body. The rituals and sacraments handed down to us work best when they are kept simple. Don't mess with them. If you do, you will only weaken them and yourself in the process. Don't do that.

CHAPTER 11

BURNT OFFERINGS

Fire transforms. The outer symbol of offering an animal as a burnt sacrifice is repugnant to us today. That's why we don't do it anymore. But, just because we have abandoned the practice doesn't mean that we should forget the principle. We take the very best we have—the first-fruits—and offer them to God. Not what we can spare, not the leftovers, not when we can or when we feel like it, but right here, right now. We offer up our highest, most exalted states of mind, our most joyful, fulfilled feelings, and our greatest victories. In short, we offer it all.

The word "sacrifice" has fallen out of favor, because it's associated with shame and the sense that there is something wrong with living a full life. Life should be enjoyed, should it not? Why would anyone want to give up a good thing? Can we buy our way into heaven? Is that the idea? Livestock was wealth in ancient times. Giving up the best of your herd was painful! Today, money is wealth. In some churches, after the collection is taken up, the basket is placed on the altar—a recapitulation of the burnt offering.

But, all of this is meaningless unless the outer symbol corresponds to an inner act. Where is the altar within us; where is the fire? And, what do we bring to it to be consumed? Everyone knows the saying, "No pain, no gain." The reason most of us don't exercise as much as we should is because it hurts. Stretching is hard; running is torture; walking is boring. This isn't true for everyone, of course, but you get my point. Advancement takes effort. Why, then, do we believe that spiritual development should come with no effort at all, as though it just happens?

So, what do we burn, and where do we burn it? Let's take an oil refinery as an example. In order to get gasoline and other refined, volatile chemicals, we heat crude oil in a tall distillation tower. As the gasses heat up, they rise higher and higher in the tower. At various points, there are bleed-off valves. The denser, cruder substances take the first available exit, while the more volatile substances keep rising. Generally speaking, the end products vary in their monetary value in direct proportion to how refined they are.

Human beings are also refineries. The fire is our life force, which rises up our spine. All along our spine are "outlets of opportunity," the lower of which have rather large openings, so to speak, while the upper ones are harder to reach. The lower openings feel good. The energy rushes out with wild abandon—quite a party, really. But, because the energy bleeds out early, all of the upward momentum is lost, and very little of real value makes it to the top.

Carolyn Myss, in her book *Anatomy of the Spirit*, gives a marvelous description of these bleed-off valves along the spine. At the lower levels, our life force expresses itself in the most tenacious, survival-oriented ways, having mostly to do with tribal attachments, procreation, and aggression. At the upper levels, it expresses more as compassion, creativity, insight, and oneness. The more we value our attachments to everyday life and its concerns, the less the upper aspects get developed. So if we value those aspects, we *sacrifice* the lower ones, at least for a time, so that the life force within us can reach the top.

When Jesus told the young rich man to sell all that he had and give to the poor, he was telling him to convert his attachments and proclivities into spiritual cash. Whether our bound-up energy is dedicated to material goods, emotional ties, sexual or culinary appetites, or whatever, the energy is just energy. It isn't "good energy" or "bad energy." It can be cashed in and converted into *useable* energy. And, as we all know, it is much easier to redirect energy than it is to stop it. Trying to stop energy is like trying to stop a locomotive— the locomotive always wins.

The "poor" that are in need of our "cash" are those aspects of ourselves that have been starved of the energy they need in order to develop. Our distractions with our career keep us so busy that we forget to meditate. Any time an emotional trigger goes off, we rush to the nearest exit (addiction) so that we don't have to face what's really going on. Our anger only serves to reinforce our need to be right, instead of galvanizing us into taking meaningful action, and on and on. There are many impoverished aspects of ourselves we could address if we weren't so fixated on how good (or how special) our lower nature makes us feel.

Our lower nature is our *animal* nature. This is the animal that has to be sacrificed in order that our higher nature can receive the energy the lower nature has been hogging. It's really a matter of redirecting the energy within us. This is the real meaning of "burnt offering" and "sacrifice." As priests, we have to know how to do that, not only for ourselves, but for others too.

As a teenager, I loved to drive fast. I had a British sports car, and I competed in many an autocross on weekends and often raced my friends around Lake Tahoe and up and down the Virginia City highway just outside of Reno, Nevada. It's a wonder that I'm still alive. Later, as I got older, I would find myself, from time to time, driving like a teenager. My work required a lot of driving, and the temptation to make it interesting was sometimes too much to resist. But, inevitably I would start to feel the long arm of the law catching up with me. I just knew that if I didn't slow down and drive the speed limit, I was sure to get a ticket. It was like a pressure building up inside of me. I discovered, however, that if I obeyed the speed limit signs, or better yet, drove *under* the speed limit, the accumulated karma would start to burn off. It felt like a spiritual fever. It was my own brand of penance—driving *slower* than what the speed limit allowed. I was "sacrificing" my need for speed so that I wouldn't have to pay for my past transgressions. I still had to pay, but it was a controlled burn, not the flash fire of a speeding ticket.

There's nothing wrong with the pleasures of life or going with the flow. Earth is a beautiful place, and the bodies we inhabit can provide us with many a joyful experience. But if we want more than just a pleasant life—if we are called to higher elevations—sacrifices must be made. It takes effort to climb out of a rut. The potential for easy pleasures can be saved up for more substantial gains. The pull of Earth's gravity can be overcome if you have enough fuel to achieve escape velocity. That pleasurable feeling in your gut can be channeled up into your head—*if you have the will*. And the fireworks can be spectacular!

If the Altar of Sacrifice hadn't been acted out in all of its physical goriness, the principle would have been lost. Some things have to be graphically demonstrated in order to make the idea stick. Today, we don't have to do that. But we do have to find that same altar within ourselves. Simply slaughtering an animal had to have been a lot easier than giving up our favorite distractions. But, inner actions have always been harder than outer ones. *N'est-ce pas?*

CHAPTER 12

SIN, ABSOLUTION, AND HEALING

Let's talk some more about priests being catalysts. A catalyst is a chemical that breaks apart a chemical compound by taking one of its components for itself. But because the new pairing with the catalyst is unstable, it quickly breaks apart.

A good example of this is the way that chlorine interacts with ozone. (Bear with me here—understanding catalytic action is essential in understanding absolution.) Ozone is a molecule of three oxygen atoms (O_3). In nature, ozone protects the Earth from harmful ultraviolet sunlight by acting as a shield in the upper atmosphere. When man-made chemicals such as chlorofluorocarbons from air-conditioners and aerosol cans are released into the air, the chlorine in them takes one of the oxygen atoms in an ozone molecule and binds with it, leaving behind a normal oxygen molecule

(O2). But because the new bond between the chlorine and oxygen atom is volatile, it quickly breaks apart, leaving the chlorine atom free to interact with yet another ozone molecule. This enables one atom of chlorine to destroy one million molecules of ozone *every minute.*

Here's the spiritual correlation: When we think negative thoughts, it changes the quality of our presence, the way we are *being* in the world. We begin to vibrate at a different frequency. Everyone can tell that there is something going on with us, that we are not ourselves. At the spiritual level, these negative thoughts have substance, just as matter has substance on the physical level. And like physical matter, this spiritual stuff acts and reacts according to the same principles as its physical counterpart. Too much negativity in a person's thinking can cause all sorts of complications, from health issues to psychological problems (just as chlorine causes problems in the upper atmosphere). Vitality suffers. As with any accumulation of negativity, the worse it gets, the worse it gets—the effects are cumulative. If it goes unchecked, negativity can disrupt our entire system, both physically and spiritually.

Priests have the ability to absorb this negativity and then release it, just like a catalyst. We do this through direct contact with a person, either by the laying on of hands or through psychic connection. It doesn't matter if we are in the physical presence of the afflicted person; mental contact is just as real. This is how Jesus was able to heal people, such as the centurion's servant, from a distance.

Human negativity is largely emotion-driven and is therefore highly volatile. It will readily discharge itself, when the conditions are right, onto any willing recipient. Well-meaning people are affected by negativity by unknowingly attuning themselves with the negative vibrations of another person. It rubs off on them. They *take on* the other person's sins, and it changes the quality of their own spiritual presence. It's important, therefore, that if you attempt to absolve someone of his or her sins, that you first learn how to do it safely. This is not as difficult as it might sound. We simply *know* that we are not the ones doing it, that it's God doing the work. We are merely the conduit—the *catalyst*—by which it happens.

"Sin," for the purposes of this discussion, is defined as a vibratory condition that interferes with a person's physical and spiritual vitality. Other definitions, such as "missing the mark," do little to help us understand the actual dynamics of this phenomenon, so it's better if we approach the subject scientifically and look at it in terms of power, force, and energy. As a vibratory condition, vitality is a state of resonance with the One Life, whereas sin is a state of dissonance. The One Life is the fundamental frequency emanating from the spiritual body of the Sun—the Christ Being—that pervades this entire Solar System. All life depends upon it for support. As long as there are intrinsic alignments, vibrationally speaking, between a life-form and its energy source (the Sun), it will thrive. But introduce a dissonant vibration, and reverberations start to occur, which can then create health problems.

We are spiritual beings, which means that we are energy first and matter second. Matter is the stuff that "hangs" on an energy matrix, the way that sand arranges itself in patterns on a paper diaphragm when you vibrate it with an electronic tone. It's the vibratory matrix that creates the pattern, not the sand. Change the matrix, and you change the visible pattern. In hierarchical terms, the vibration is "superior" to the pattern. It *rules* it.

The primary source of vibration in this Solar System is the Sun. It's vibrations create a standing field in the space that surrounds it extending to the farthest reaches of its boundaries, the heliopause. What is a "standing field"? If you drop a pebble into a body of water, the displacement will create ripples. The ripples will radiate outward in concentric rings as they spend the energy of the pebble's impact with the surface of the water. But if you vibrate a liquid in a container, say a bowl of water sitting on top of a stereo speaker, the sound vibrations will cause the surface of the water to ripple in stationary patterns. The concentric rings will stay in their positions and not travel to the rim of the bowl. Vary the frequency of the sound, and the rings will arrange themselves accordingly—immediately and precisely.

Our physical and spiritual bodies are constituted in the same way. They are held in place by the frequencies emanating from the center of our being. The patterns are infinitely more complex, of course, much more so than the ripples in a bowl of water, but in principle they are the same thing. Any disturbances in the vibratory matrix are going to affect our entire physical and spiritual system. When we allow intense negative thinking into our vibrational makeup, we alter the patterns of the flow of life's energy through us. This is called "interference." When such a condition is allowed to persist, long-term damage will result.

We are not the creators of our own vibratory makeup. We can affect it with our thinking, but we are not the architects of its fundamental structure. God is. In Christian mystical language, the fundamental architecture of human being is called the "Son/Sun of Man." The Sun is the first manifestation of the intelligence of our local cosmos. Its energy holds our spiritual vehicles in their designated patterns by feeding and resonating with the Solar Pattern within our own being. Christian mystics throughout history have been keenly aware of this spiritual form. Saint Paul called it the "celestial body."

These greater patterns do not necessarily look the same at different scales, but in principle they are identical. The principles never change, but the outward forms continually evolve. Evolution is the keyword here, because unless we understand human being as a *dynamic* constellation of vibratory patterns, we cannot heal the problems that beset it. Healing is the process of reinforcing the Solar Pattern of the Son/Sun of Man so that it can purge itself of the patterns of interference created by our negative thinking.

Priests do not have to be perfect in and of themselves in order to heal others or absolve people of their sins, no more than a midwife has to deliver the baby through her own body. Priests do not have to fully embody the Solar Pattern, but they do have to be able to *access* it, and they have to be able to connect it to the person they are healing. They have the authority to mediate the necessary energies, which realign and strengthen the Solar Pattern within an individual. The revitalized spiritual (celestial) body can then purge *itself* of the harmful effects of negative thinking.

"Sin" is an archaic word—we really should get rid of it. It keeps us from understanding that it is a condition and not a fundamental flaw in the design of human being. Creation is God's self-exploration, the engine of which is possibility. In order for possibility to exist, there must also be the possibility for making mistakes. You can't have one without the other—that's the trade-off. Free will has its purpose in this divine scheme. It is the one thing that makes growth and development possible, because unless our choices arise from within us unbidden and unscripted by others, they do not benefit us spiritually. We do not get to heaven by merely following the rules. We get there when we take heaven into our hearts. Righteousness comes when we desire to *be* righteous, not when we act righteously because we're afraid of what will happen if we don't.

Right action must be spontaneous before it can be *right action.*

CHAPTER 13

COMMUNION

To understand the way spiritual power manifests in the physical world, we must first grasp the principle of mediation. In order for a higher energy to interact with a lower energy, there has to be a mediating agent—an *interface*—something that resonates harmonically with both the above and the below.

Our soul, for instance, is of a higher nature, vibrationally speaking, than our physical body. At the same time, it is of a lower nature than God. The soul is the medium through which divine energies feed into our physical body. But just as this is true in principle, it must also be true in the physical—there has to be a physical counterpart, a *correlation*, through which real energy can produce real results.

If we look for the correlation in our physical body, we find that it is our blood that mediates between us and the world. Blood carries oxygen from the air we breathe and nutrients from the food we eat. It delivers these elements to the cells of our body. It also carries away the waste products of our metabolism, the toxic gasses released by our cells as they process these substances.

Both oxygen and the broken-down molecules of food are more volatile than the dense, stabilized molecules of our flesh and bones. They are the "above," in terms of vibration, to the "below" of these bodily structures. And the blood mediates between them.

Blood is the central theme in Christian symbolism. It winds its way through the entire story of Jesus Christ, from his bloodline connection to the House of David to the spilling of his blood at the crucifixion. But comparing the story of Jesus to the physiological significance of physical blood is not just an analogy, neither is it an attempt to mythicize the story of Christ's passion. It is neither an analogy nor a myth—it is a *correlation*. That which is in heaven is *mirrored* in that which is in Earth. And it is this mirroring that provides the resonant *form* through which spiritual energies can bridge the gap between heaven and Earth.

The physical substance of blood carries the spiritual vibrations of the heaven worlds—the intelligence and characteristics of our soul. Just as our soul is in continuous contact with God, so is our blood in continuous contact with our soul, primarily through the air we breathe (*pneuma, ruach, spirit, prana*). And in turn, our physical structure, our body, is in continual contact with our blood. Correlation. These systems are nested within each other; they form an unbroken chain from the Godhead to our being in the world.

- God
- Soul
- Blood
- Body

We bring Earth and heaven together by offering ourselves as the interface. When we live in the world as a soul and Self, it is our blood that carries the vibration of those essential qualities. It is our blood that acts like an antenna that continually transmits spiritual frequencies into our flesh, which in turn radiates those qualities into the space around us.

Reach up through the octaves of your being and feel the spiritual presence within your blood—the light, the consciousness, the *Christ*. This is where your life is! When you focus your attention there, you are inviting the Christ Being into your body. Your blood is your point of connection.

We are so used to thinking of ourselves as the image we see in the mirror—a body covered with skin. It feels inert, almost lifeless. This is *not* who we are. Even if you wholeheartedly believe that you are *only* your body, you would be selling yourself short to think that you are only what you can see with your physical eyes, as though you had no organs, no skeletal system, and no *blood*.

It is the heart, the lungs, and the blood coursing through our arteries that are much more real than our skin, our appearance. Why? Because that's where all the action is! Our blood never stops moving; it pumps through our heart with great *force*. As it moves through our lungs, it changes color and emerges bright and clean. This is our LIFE, our soul characteristics, and the Spirit energies that flow through them. Our blood glows with US! This is why the word *pneuma* is used for the soul; it is the life breath, the oxygen in our blood infused with the light of the great Christ Being. This is who and *what* we really are.

Blood carries the consciousness. It is the medium through which the life body enters into the physical plane. By bringing the light of Christ down into it, we purge it of everything that is not of Christ. This happens instantaneously and completely, although through mis-thinking we can recreate the corruption just as quickly. But, each time an infusion takes place, it brings us closer to a complete and permanent transformation.

The bread is the body and what we do with it—the form. It is the Substance we consume. Bread is made in an oven, the alchemical furnace called *Athenor*. This means that it is through our actions, the subjugation of our lower impulses to our reason that the body is prepared as a fitting vessel for the light of Christ. Sacrificing our personal will purifies it by and through the agency of alchemical Fire (read Hebrews 10). As we release it, our karma is burned up: *know that through the fruits of your labors that you are absolved of all past error.*

If we are to be the agents of absolution through the sacrament of Communion, we have to be really clear about the true nature of right and wrong and not let our ideas get in the way of the movement of the Spirit as it flows through us to the recipient. The Spirit knows, so we don't have to. Absolution is a movement of *power*, not the utterance of a few prescribed words. It is power that transmutes karma, not ideas.

Right and wrong do not necessarily mean whether our actions conform to an external set of rules. It has a more immediate and pertinent meaning when we consider that it's the small, everyday choices we make that determine whether we will succeed or fail on the spiritual path. Following God's will, then, means listening to the still, small voice within us, not the written laws that are so subject to interpretation. Our own inner guidance is what we need to follow, not the ideas written in our heads—the oughts and shoulds that more often than not exercise authority over us like a cruel, unforgiving dictator.

At the soul level, we know that God is a living being, an omnipresent reality that lives within us and within whom we live. We know it right now. It is a knowledge that we are born with but one we keep hidden, even from ourselves. It takes only the smallest effort on our part—especially when we are engaged in sacred ritual such as the Communion—to connect with that inner part of us. We let it take over. We let it speak through us, and we let the form of the ritual speak its own language through our whole body.

On the surface, the Communion ritual is about the common meal, a community of believers sharing their daily bread. It can also be a metaphor for partaking of the same beliefs, the same lifestyle, and the same divine reality. But there is another aspect, one that is easily overlooked—the act itself and what it means to *eat*.

What does it take to swallow your food? What does the body have to *know* in order to allow a substance to pass through the mouth and down the esophagus? There has to be a system-wide acceptance of what is eaten, even before it enters the mouth. The food has to pass multiple tests in the way of flavor, texture, and freshness before the body will swallow it. A lot goes on in the act of eating. Without the tacit cooperation of our body, eating can be nearly impossible. We will gag unless the body is receptive to the food we put into our mouths.

Every physical action has a spiritual correlate. Walking is an expression of our will to move from one state of consciousness to another. Reaching out our hand is an expression of either what we want or what we are willing to accept. Sitting is an act of situating ourselves at the stillpoint of our being. What does eating express? It expresses the act of *transmuting* the world.

By taking food, we assume that it is compatible with our being. Our bodies are literally formed out of the substances we put into them. In a sense, we eat that which we already are.

Normally, we do this unconsciously, out of habit. We eat because we need to, and we don't really give the act itself much thought, unless there's a problem. We hardly ever consider its spiritual aspect. When we sense that there's been a divine influx into the elements of the Communion, the bread and wine, and we feel the presence of the Christ in our midst, the physical act of eating these things is a proclamation with our entire being, from the physical to the spiritual, that what we are experiencing is what we *already are*. There is a fundamental resonance with the deepest part of our spiritual selves that enables us to willingly reach out and incorporate more of it into our being. *We make the outer as the inner and the inner as the outer.*

Swallowing our food is the summation of our acceptance of it, the last line of demarcation, the crossing of which requires a commitment on our part to be transformed. We are not used to thinking of ourselves as energy beings, but when the gate of our esophagus opens, our entire energetic structure changes. We go from maintaining our current energy state to allowing something to pass through it. Once the food is swallowed, we go back to being our vigilant selves, and our electromagnetic defenses snap back into place.

It matters little whether we believe that an actual transmutation has taken place in the bread and wine *if* we regard them as symbolic of the Person of Christ. That's what we're going for anyway, right? It's the *Person*, not the flesh and blood, that we want to incorporate. Besides, what would the body and blood of an ascended being consist of? Certainly, it would be an energetic substance, not a physical one. And yet, when we accept these new vibrations into our blood, the soul characteristics of Jesus Christ, our flesh is changed. This is why the sacrament of Communion is repeatable. Over time, the transformation of our flesh continues until it is complete—the *resurrection* of our physical body from its entropic descent into the tomb of matter.

The body and the blood of Christ are his intelligence and his consciousness. His intelligence is the record of his experiences while on Earth—the Way. His consciousness is his moment-by-moment oneness with God, his dynamic attunement with the Great Being. This is what we desire to consume. This is what we want to become. And we don't want to merely suspend it above the altar or hold it in mind as an ideal. No. We want to enter into it, and we want it to enter into us.

The Communion is real. It is real in a way that does not conform with the average person's ideas about it. It is not a concept, nor is it a memorial. How could it be a memorial if it is a *living* reality? Even though the substance of the Communion is spiritual, the act of receiving it brings the Spirit into physical manifestation, the same way that food is turned into our physical flesh. We are spiritual (energy) beings having a physical experience, as the saying goes. And who knows where one begins and the other ends? Twirled into one, they cannot be undone.

CHAPTER 14

HOW TO CONDUCT YOURSELF AT THE ALTAR

Our first duty as priests in performing the sacraments is to make the space we are occupying *sacred*. Our entire consciousness must be filled with God. Whether we are working in the sanctuary of a cathedral or on a nightstand in a hospital room, our atmosphere must be *charged* with the Divine Presence. No physical object, no matter how sanctified, can compensate for the lack of the focused intention of a conscious priest.

The more they are used for sacred purposes, so-called "sacred spaces" and their implements become energized with the power of Spirit. This is why we don't treat them like ordinary objects. It is for this reason that we handle them with reverence. But that's all; they have no power in and of themselves. They are symbols of a long tradition, and as such they warrant our due respect. We don't wear robes, for instance, because *we ourselves* are holy, but because of what they symbolize—the Priesthood.

Putting on robes for a public service makes a statement. It says that we are there representing something larger than ourselves. It places an added responsibility on us to deliver the power of the Word, not our opinions. When we put on our robes, we put on the Priesthood in its public expression. What we do and say will reflect on all priests, not just us as individuals. This is not to say that we have to be sterile or impersonal. On the contrary, it means that we had better be coming from the heart more than from the mind. After all, people don't usually remember what you say, but they *always* remember how you made them feel. Let them feel the presence of God.

What we do at the altar matters. Our every action should be performed with the consciousness of God. After all, it is God's altar, not ours. How we move and the actions we take are as much a part of our language as the words we speak. So, we need to understand what our movements and actions mean.

For instance, what's the difference between kneeling and standing? Both actions are living symbols. When we kneel, we declare our helplessness and utter dependence on God for our very life. God is the One Source of All, and by kneeling, we surrender to God's power. *Do with me as Thou wilt.* Kneeling is passive. It is receptive. It is *negative.* We are making ourselves smaller than, shorter than, weaker than. We are saying to God, "I am willing to receive. I am *asking* for your blessing." Like water, power flows "downhill." And by kneeling, we symbolically increase the differential between God and us. Besides, kneeling makes it easier to *look up.*

What about standing? When we raise the chalice from a standing position, it feels different than when we raise it while kneeling. To understand why, we have to know what standing symbolizes. To stand means to *embody.* It is to allow the forces to gather around you and infuse themselves into your structure. Remember, they are not your forces—you did not create God—but by standing, you *take on* the power of God through the Great Christos. You become the transformed and transfigured Lord Jesus Christ.

To stand is to create a kind of centripetal force. All of the powers of nature swirl around you, ready to do your bidding. Devotion has set the stage and purified your intention. Now, with love as your guide, you exercise the prerogative given to us by our Creator. You speak the Word of Power.

Does this sound egotistical or occult? Let me ask you this: why are you there if not to *do something?* Besides, if you start to think that *you* are powerful, then look out! You are going to have nothing but problems. But, if you know that it is God's power—that you take it on in the same impersonal way that you put on your priestly vestments—then you are ready to function as a priest. You are ready to do the work of planetary transformation by *being* an agent of the Christ Being.

One of the great secrets of the Priesthood is that you have to bring heaven to Earth. You have to provide the *form* in order for Spirit to manifest. It doesn't all happen in your head! What you bind on earth is bound in heaven. Priests are not afraid to get their hands dirty. Kneeling requires reaching up. Standing allows you to realize that you *already have* that for which you are reaching. Experiment with both. Learn how each one feels. Then you will know the difference and when to use one or the other.

The more we approach the altar with reverence and a sense of awe, the stronger the pattern becomes, and the easier it will be to invoke the power of the Spirit to take action in the world. Spiritual tools become sharper the more we use them. They become more effective the more we put them to a task. The Spirit *loves* to work, to heal, and to do good. But it acts with precision, so we must be focused when we approach this work.

Make your chapel a sacred space. The more you dedicate it to the worship of God, the more your priestly work will be effective. And, if you don't have the luxury of a sacred space, cultivate your personal atmosphere so that you can invoke the Divine Presence wherever you are.

CHAPTER 15

FORM—DON'T LET THE MEDIUM BECOME THE MESSAGE

We have to watch ourselves that we don't get caught up in the glamor of liturgy and the paraphernalia of our tradition. When we do, we lose the intention for which these forms were established. The tendency is to dress up the simple, to adorn the elegant, to customize the original. Simple formulae tend to devolve into statements of individual style and/or religious identification. And the message, the *transmission*, gets lost beneath the overlay.

Jesus built his church on the transmission of truth, not on established lineages and outer forms of worship. The transmission is the carrier wave, the power within the tradition, but the uninitiated can easily mistake the outer trappings as the source of that power, what little of it can still be detected underneath the glitter. We need the form, but we must not exalt it above the transmission. *Not ever.* The form was made to serve the transmission, not the other way around.

Jesus once asked his students, "Whom do men say that I the Son of man am?" They had various answers: John the Baptist, Elias, Jeremias. "But whom say *ye* that I am,» he persisted. Peter said, «Thou art the Christ, the Son of the living God.» Jesus replied, «Blessed art thou, Simon Barjona, for flesh and blood hath not revealed it unto thee, but my Father which is in heaven. And I say also unto thee, that thou art Peter, and upon this rock I will build my church; and the gates of hell shall not prevail against it."

The name "Peter" comes from the Greek word "petros," which means "rock." Up until this point, Peter's name had been "Cephas," which means "pebble." Now, "Cephas" is the diminutive of the name "Caiaphas," which was the name of the Jewish High Priest at the time. So on one level, we could say that Jesus was replacing the current High Priest with one of his own, but on a deeper level we can say that getting one's answers from within is the "rock" that forms the basis of the Priesthood. The energy of Life (and the intelligence that informs it) fills every cubic centimeter of space in this Solar System. What could be more solid than that? Real authority comes from God, not through forms, temples, or official titles.

At that time in history, the term "Son of God" was in widespread use. Caesar was a "Son of God," for instance. Sons of God were understood to be Sun gods, such as Ra, Apollo, and Helios. It was understood then, as it is today, that the Sun is the source and sustainer of all life. So, Jesus' question to Peter, in which he identifies himself as the "Son of man," can be restated like this: The life energy of human beings, that which animates us and gives us our vitality—is it a product of our biological chemistry? Does it originate within each individual's physical body? Or, is it a universal energy having its origin in the great creative intelligence we call God?

By asking the question this way, we can infer two characteristics of the phenomenon we call "life." One is that life is a *power*, and two, that that power is *intelligent*. It creates the forms it needs for its own self-expression. Life builds its forms from within—it *in-forms* them for its own purposes and explorations. The closer we get to that life, the closer we get to the intelligence that informs it. Or we can say it this way: the closer we get to the Son/Sun, the closer we get to the Father Who sent him. We know of ourselves *as we live*. Our intuitions are proven by our activity, not by how good they sound as ideas.

The scribes and Pharisees knew the letter of the Law. They knew all the rules. But they had lost the transmission of the living reality that their teachings pointed to. Buddha had stated 500 years before that he was merely the finger pointing *at* the moon, not the moon itself. The Jewish hierarchy had also lost their compassion—they were fixated on the mind and had lost touch with their hearts. Human needs had become irrelevant; the only thing that mattered was strict adherence to the Law. Such is the tendency of an intellect untempered by love.

The liturgy of religion, along with all of its trappings, is nothing without feeling. The power of life must move through them before they can come *alive*. When we spend too much energy debating which form is correct or which color robes we should wear, we block the movement of the Spirit. The forms are the *intelligence* of our work, but without the heart the forms are dead.

When we feel the movement of the Spirit, its energy will show us what is correct. We will know just as surely as if we were experimenting with electrical circuits—an application either works or it doesn't. Let that be the criteria for all of the forms you use. At the same time, realize that even though the forms that are available to us today are probably buried under layers of add-ons and cultural inflections, the core elements are there if we look for them. But it's going to take a down-to-earth simplicity and a basic understanding of the laws of physics to find them. The bottom-line is whether they work—do they transform people, or do they (because they are familiar) merely keep them comfortable?

Our goal as priests is to *become* the sacraments here in this life. Our very presence should be transformative to all those around us. Can you manifest the Body and the Blood while standing in the checkout line at the grocery store? This is the test—*become* the form. "And may I become the transformed and transfigured Lord Jesus Christ." "This is my body—this is my blood." If Jesus came simply to turn wine into blood, where would be the grace in that? That would only be magic—the direction of force outward onto the world. Nothing in us would be transformed at all.

PART 3

TOOLS OF THE TRADE

CHAPTER 16

RENUNCIATION

We are awash with the world, saturated by it. From the moment we wake up in the morning until we go to bed at night, our cares and concerns fill our consciousness and shape our thoughts. No wonder we feel so powerless in the face of world events and human interactions. The Priesthood is about changing all of that. It's about carving out a space in the clutter, about creating an eye in the storm of the world's circumstances, and finding a stillpoint for humanity's self-awareness.

This is the meaning and purpose of renunciation in the life of a priest. It's one thing to be engaged with life and all of its normal arrangements—family, job, friendships, entertainments—and quite another to be caught in life's thrall. Nothing saps our strength like distraction. Renunciation, on the other hand, is the power to say no, not just to this or that, but to *everything*. It is an intentional clearing of the space around us, both physical space and psychic space. It is what in the Upanishads is called, «*neti neti* « (not this, not that), the complete rejection of the contents of the mind as a means of creating a clearing in which reality can show up.

Obviously, this is difficult to maintain and still be a functioning member of society. But, it is a necessary skill to have in order to be a functioning priest. This is not to say that life is bad or evil; it is simply a way to clear out our misinterpretations, the ones that tend to accumulate and distort what's really in front of us, especially the ideas we have about other people and ourselves. "Nothing is good or bad but thinking makes it so," said William Shakespeare. Renunciation is a way to bring our ideas about reality back to zero.

Our senses are constantly being solicited by the world around us, its stimuli crowding in like street market hawkers. Unless priests can draw a circle of emptiness around themselves when confronted with the sheer impact of Earth life, they cannot be effective agents of change. They will simply be just another part of the world. And the world needs priests, like the body needs white blood cells. Because nothing threatens life on Earth more than people with ironclad assumptions, and the very presence of a functioning priest can blow those assumptions apart.

Ironically, it takes humility to rise above the rest of humanity, because no one attains spiritually by looking down on others. Unless you love people, you cannot be an effective priest. To love others despite their imperfections requires a certain audacity, because such a love violates every instinct of the ego. It takes boldness to pierce through one's own judgments.

Boldness does not succeed by permission, neither do you establish a stillpoint by consensus. Unless you can stand in the Holy Place, which is to say *Self,* no transformation will take place around you. The world will fight you on this; it will challenge your every attempt to rise above it. And don't think that you can do this covertly—"a city on a hill cannot be hid"—everyone will see you. They will fight you tooth and nail and will continually try to get you back into the fold in order to validate themselves. If you resist their attempts, they will reject you. But, we can take comfort in Jesus' words, "Blessed are ye, when men shall revile you, and persecute you, and shall say all manner of evil against you falsely, for my sake. Rejoice, and be exceeding glad: for great is your reward in heaven: for so persecuted they the prophets which were before you."

Merely being ordained a priest does not raise you above the world. There are plenty of priests who are completely embroiled in their attempts to please others. And neither do you need to be a priest to practice renunciation. But if you do practice it, and your motives are pure, the Priesthood will come to you almost by default. You will get the attention of those above, because you're the kind of person they're looking for. Heaven's task is to raise the consciousness of humanity, and it will use any available opportunity to do so.

How does renunciation work? Simply stated, "Nature abhors a vacuum." When we create a space around us, we set up an immediate potential—an empty space. No doubt you have seen this demonstrated many times in your life. Any time you see people who command authority, people who cannot be swayed by popular opinion and who are not easily swept away by the emotions of others, you are seeing people who have mastered this skill. They are renunciates. They have the ability to say no to the world. Consequently, the world tends to move around *them*, and not the other way around.

Priests do not have to be leaders, not in a worldly sense, but they must never be followers—not in *any* sense. Priests are accountable only to God, which is, unfortunately, why so many of them have been killed throughout history; standing on principle is a lot like standing on the edge of a cliff. This is why it is so important to know the true nature of our calling, that it is not worldly power we are after, but rather to be servants of heaven—*"My kingdom is not of this world."* Renunciation, in the worldly sense, is to renounce worldly gain—personal wealth and political influence. It's not that you cannot have these things, it's that they must never have *you*. We all have to be in the world, but we must never be *of* it. To be a priest is to be a cause, not an effect.

Renunciation is a principle—a law—an aspect of the Priesthood. It acts like a filter, a barrier through which only that which is real can pass. Without it, you will be so infused with the world's mind that you will be indistinguishable from it.

Knowing God is a process of elimination. As we reject everything that our intellect wants us to believe, we set up a force field in the mind, a force field that destroys all that is not eternal. God cannot be slain; we cannot destroy that which is real. Truth is forever the enemy of falsehood, so we need not fear losing anything of spiritual value. When it comes to emptying our mind, the baby can never be thrown out with the bathwater. The mind cannot throw itself out, only its contents. When the particulate matter (our thoughts) settles to the bottom, the water (our mind) is clear, and sunlight illuminates the whole body.

Our thoughts about God are just that—*thoughts.* They are mental constructs that serve us for a time but must eventually be discarded. In the words of the 9th Century Zen master, Linji Lixuan, "Followers of the Way, if you want to get the kind of understanding that accords with the Dharma, never be misled by others. Whether you're facing inward or facing outward, whatever you meet up with, just kill it! If you meet a buddha, kill the buddha. If you meet a patriarch, kill the patriarch. If you meet an arhat, kill the arhat. If you meet your parents, kill your parents. If you meet your kinfolk, kill your kinfolk. Then for the first time you will gain emancipation, will not be entangled with things, will pass freely anywhere you wish to go."

Obviously, Linji is not telling his students to *literally* kill their families, just as Jesus wasn't telling his disciples to literally hate theirs. What has to die is our *concepts* about the things we hold important, and the attachments we have to them. Our concepts are only there to help us find the experience of the reality they signify. They are the "finger pointing at the moon, not the moon."

There comes a point in everyone's spiritual progress where they must "kill" their concepts. There are vast numbers of seekers gathered at the temple gates worshipping commonly accepted mental images of God, staring at the pictures, enraptured by their beauty, preferring their beautiful ideas over the reality they portray. They are stuck there, caught up in their ideas *about* God, holding onto them either because of pride or out of fear, either afraid to admit there is something greater than themselves or that they will lose their place in line if they simply let go.

Our own self-image is also a thought. We must be willing to sacrifice our "self," the small-s self, so that our larger *Self* can express. This requires a kind of EMP (electromagnetic pulse), a global reset button in the brain, something that can clear the cache and leave us with a virginal consciousness. Some people pursue this with alcohol or drugs and sometimes with an overdose of adrenaline, putting themselves in dangerous situations so that they can "live in the moment," to find out who they "really are." But, it's far better to do it yourself with intention and willpower. Will, after all, is the polar opposite of ego.

The egoist always overestimates his abilities, and the willful rarely reflect before they act. This is why the ancient temples of initiation had two pillars at their entrance, symbolizing ego and will. In Solomon's Temple, they were called "Jachin and Boaz." All candidates for the Mysteries first had to demonstrate that they could walk the "middle path" between these two forces of the mind—form vs. content, image vs. power—before they could "go within" and then proceed "behind the veil."

They had to prove that they could walk willingly into a fiery furnace, like the three Jews in Babylonian exile in the Book of Daniel—Shadrach, Meshach, and Abednego. They had to show themselves willing to offer themselves on the cross of Golgotha, the "place of the skull," as Jesus did, hanging between the two thieves, condemned to die before he could enter the kingdom of heaven. Each of these stories is a formula for achieving spiritual balance, involving three factors—the candidate, his will, and his ego.

When God told Moses to "...put off thy shoes from off thy feet, for the place whereon thou standest is holy ground," it was an injunction to leave the world and its ideas at the door, the same way we do when we enter a chapel or meditation room. Similarly, Jesus told his disciples to "shake off the dust of your feet," to put the criticisms and ridicule of others out of their minds before proceeding on their journeys. Both of these examples imply a certain level of mastery over one's thoughts, the ability to clear one's field of consciousness so that God's mind can be revealed.

Ordinary acts of renunciation, like a child giving up candy during Lent or an adult taking a temporary vow of celibacy, are useful as teaching tools. They develop one's spiritual muscles. But, they are not the realities they point to. They are *practices* designed to help us overcome the will of the flesh. Far more adversarial is the will of the mind—the thought-patterns handed down genetically in the form of neural pathways in the human brain.

With God, all things are possible. Just look at the extraordinary feats of physical mastery on YouTube, everything from doing backflips thirty feet in the air on a motorcycle to four-year-olds playing the drums, and you will see that we have collectively mastered the physical body to unprecedented degrees. The flesh does not willingly give itself to such extremes. So, it is high time we cut to the chase and practice renunciation in the way Linji and Jesus describe it—to ruthlessly slay our concepts of reality so that *reality itself* can show up in all of its life-affirming potential.

This is an upgrade to the Law of Renunciation. The outer forms are no longer as important as they were in the past. And though none of us feels like we are ready to let go of those forms, we have to. Otherwise, the forms themselves will prevent any further progress. This doesn't mean we can do whatever our appetites dictate, not at all. It means that it no longer works to simply obey the rules by force of will. We have to exercise the principle of renunciation *in our thinking*.

It is our thoughts that shape our lives now, much more than our actions. Why? Because our thoughts determine which actions we will take. We can no longer rely on established patterns of tradition, because the world is changing faster than traditions can keep up. We must instead train ourselves to think properly, to consciously question the appearance of things, to apply principle to our perceptions, and to discern truth for ourselves. We cannot simply say that something is true because that's the way it's always been done. Neither can we define truth as that which everyone believes. And, we cannot get to that point by using the same mind that got us to those erroneous conclusions in the first place. "Be ye transformed by the renewing of your mind," said Saint Paul. *Throw out* your old concepts, and give God a clean slate upon which to write God's Laws *as God sees them*, not as you understand them to be!

CHAPTER 17

THE NATURE OF ENERGY

A woman once told me that she had trouble meditating. Every time she closed her eyes and went within, her body would start to sway back and forth in a circular kind of way. It would get so bad that she felt as though she would fall over. The feeling was uncomfortable, so she preferred to simply sit still with her eyes open and just get quiet.

I suggested that the next time she tried to meditate, she could try a visualization I had used that might calm things down. I told her to see a straight line, perfectly vertical, running right up her spine. At the same time, she was to visualize another straight line passing through the center of her body and extending directly in front and behind, extending outward indefinitely. Along with this, she was to visualize a third straight line passing through the same center extending to the left and right. The next time I saw her, she told me that by using this visualization only one time, the swaying problem had completely disappeared. She had no trouble meditating from that time on.

We are energy beings. Energy moves through us continually. We don't have to conjure it up or try to generate it; it is always there. Sometimes, as in the case with this woman, it can feel as though there is too much energy coursing through us, so we need to learn how to stabilize it.

Each astrological age has a symbol that describes the nature of the energy prevalent in that age. In the Age of Taurus, for example, divine power was symbolized as a bull. It was an agrarian era, and cattle were the "horsepower" of the day. Students were taught to cultivate a calm and steady use of spiritual power, harnessing it so that natural forces could be directed towards the arts, turning everyday items into lovely expressions of opulence and beauty. Out of this idea of harnessing divine energy came the practice of yoga, which in Sanskrit means *yoke*.

Then, in the Age of Aries, spiritual energy was channeled into physical prowess, athletic skill, the martial arts, and war. The emphasis was on swift, decisive *action*, almost the polar opposite of the slow and steady Taurus energy. Later came the Age of Pisces, which was the discovery and deciphering of the living energies of the subconscious. The emphasis shifted away from the physical world to the kingdom of heaven, and the idea of losing one's familiar identity to plumb the depths of the unseen worlds was out-pictured in asceticism and monastic disciplines.

Now we are in the Age of Aquarius, where spiritual energy itself is the focus. The symbol for Aquarius is a man pouring out a jar of water, the glyph for which is two wavy lines. The wavy lines symbolize vibration. More specifically, they represent *airwaves*, the lines of force created by electromagnetism.

We use vibrations to accomplish many different kinds of tasks. Ultrasound, for example, can enable us to see inside a human body, or it can be used to physically break up bits of matter. High frequency energies tend to *disrupt* existing states, such as molecules, calcium deposits, and even *governments* (thus Aquarius' reputation for being revolutionary). Raise the vibration of anything, be it a body, an idea, or an emotion, and you immediately begin to change it. High frequencies tend to *dissolve* and *transform* anything they encounter.

The glyph for Uranus, Aquarius' ruling planet, is very similar to a cross-section of the human spinal cord, showing that the electrical nature of nerve energy is at the core of life's expression through human activity. We hear the terms "energy blockages" and "resistance" used to describe how energy flows through us and how we can remove the restrictions we have placed in its path. In meditation, for instance, the energy flowing through our body can itself tell us the correct posture to assume. Energy and the way it moves becomes the way shower, sometimes overturning established customs and practices of the previous ages through innovation and reform. We use whatever *works*.

Whereas in the Age of Pisces the emphasis was on the discovery of the deep currents and eddies of spiritual energies far below the surface of our awareness, now we are bringing these same energies into the light of day, to put them to use in our everyday activities, to spiritualize our lives by bringing the power of God into everything we do.

This not only applies to the way we meditate, but also to the ways in which we make our living, our relationships, and our politics—all the things that relate to us as human beings.

Just as we have harnessed the power of electricity to change our lives, so too must we learn to set patterns of thought and deed, so that we give life to those things we want to see manifested in our world —"Become the change you want to see," as Gandhi put it. Action for action's sake is no longer enough; now our actions have to be directed by reason—the rule of law for the good of all, where all are treated equally and are expected to abide by the same laws as everyone else.

This is the spirit of the Age of Aquarius, into which we are now entering. Our success is dependent upon how well we learn to control the spiritual energies of mind—our thoughts, and our attention. As priests, we must understand and *use* these new forms of energy in our Priesthood, so that we can keep up and be in harmony with this shift in the spiritual environment.

CHAPTER 18

THE SON/SUN OF GOD

In this Aquarian Age, we are literally on fire with electrical nerve energy. A full-body Kirlian photograph would be truly amazing. The problem is that most of the time we are unaware of the energy vessel that we are. Those who are aware are capable of energizing everything and everyone around them. Healers, speakers, artists—they electrify us with the power of life that radiates through their presence.

Nerve energy, the actual chemical cascade that runs back and forth through the network of nerve fibers in our body, is not itself what we're talking about here. Just as the electricity coming out of a wall socket is not that interesting, spiritually speaking, neither are the electrical impulses of the human nervous system. Both are merely mechanical phenomena. What is interesting (and *real*) about nerve energy is that it is harmonically resonant with the energy of life itself.

Just as striking middle C on a piano keyboard will cause the C's of the other octaves to resonate with sympathetic vibrations, the electrical nerve energy in our body is able to synchronize with the Light of Christ, the all-pervasive intelligent power of God that fills this Solar System. This is why we say that we are "created" by God. The life in us is resonant with—*is a response to*—the greater life of the spiritual body of the Sun. "We love because He first loved us," says the Apostle Paul—we are born into an already existing spiritual reality.

When we recognize that our life energy is simultaneously both our own and *not* our own, manifesting God in our personal life becomes possible. Life happens through us, but it also happens because we are available. We are life's oppor(tune)ity—we are in *tune* with the greater life that shines in and through us. Making the connection between the particular and the universal is what the spiritual life is all about. As above, so below. The particular is the apparatus of our physical vehicle, our body. The universal is the radiant life force, which is the vector for the intelligence of the Mind of God.

Light is a force, but it also carries information. What we call "archetypes" are discrete aspects, divine ideas, encoded within the force of life itself. Our bodies are configured the same way. The force of the electrical nerve energy is encoded with instructions from the brain. What we picture in our mind is translated by our body as specific instructions for specific reactions. Each organ has its own frequency, its own "personality," if you will. It vibrates with a particular kind of intelligence. That particular kind of intelligence is both a product of and is in *sympathetic resonance* with that part of the greater body of God. For us, the body of God is this Solar System. This is why in astrology different organs are related to different planets. The planets themselves, like the electricity that comes out of a wall socket, are not the generators of the intelligence but are merely the gross, visible part of the body of God. If we could take a Kirlian photograph of the Solar System, that would be amazing indeed!

We literally, like fish in the ocean, swim in a sea of energy. But like the fish, we have no cognizance of this fact. When we become aware that the life in us is the Life of God, then we become truly alive.

> *An eye in a blue face saw an eye in a green*
> *face. That eye is like to this eye, said the first*
> *eye. But in low place, not in high place.*

This is a riddle from The Hobbit, by J.R.R. Tolkien. The eye in a blue face is the sun; the eye in a green face is a daisy in a grassy field. We are the mirror image of that Eye, created in Its likeness. We are a step-down transformer for the life of God. Every thought we have is in some form a reflection of the Mind of God. Without that Mind, we could not think at all.

See your body for what it is—a Temple of God. The candles on the altar symbolize the Fire of Life in you. That fire reaches all the way up to heaven and all the way down to hell, from the spiritual to the profane. There is no place where God is not. When you realize that the life in you is the Life of God, and by "realize" I mean FEEL it, then your whole body will be full of light. When you see the *one thing*, that there is only One Life, that the kingdom of God is not divided against itself, then heaven will manifest before your very eyes.

Unless and until we can see God operating in our own physical body, we cannot attain spiritual realization. The spiritual path, including the Priesthood, is not merely an intellectual exercise. God cannot be experienced in books. We have to *nail* the Spirit to the cross of matter, to bring heaven down to Earth, before transformation can take place. The only way to do this is to work with the energies of life, to see life everywhere, and to learn how to direct these energies in constructive ways. Walk the talk. *Manifest* God in your life.

CHAPTER 19

SYMBOLS

The use of symbols is an integral part of the Priesthood. They are the shorthand of priestcraft. They speak directly to the subconscious mind, and they motivate the energies that well up from its depths. We work with the three basic symbols: the circle, the triangle, and the square. These energetic patterns form the basis of all sacred ritual. It's important, therefore, that we learn something about them.

The Circle

The circle with a dot in the center is an ancient symbol for God. But since God is beyond human conception, how can anything symbolize God? This is the problem the Greeks and Romans encountered in their ancient mystery schools. Instead of talking about God, they talked about God's *aspects*. They assigned names and personalities to them. Thus we have the "gods," such as Zeus, Apollo, Athena, Hera, Mars, Venus, and so on. Stories of their adventures with each other were symbolic descriptions of the relationships between different natural and metaphysical laws.

First, we must realize that geometry is not simply lines drawn on paper. Geometry is a description of the movement of power, force, and energy. As Plato said, "God always geometrizes." If you've ever used a magnifying glass to start a fire, you know that a circle with a dot in the center is more than symbolic. It is the power of concentration in action. Our mind works the same way. When we focus our attention on an idea, the process of creation begins. Thus, the circle with a dot in the center is not a symbol for God as such, but rather it is a symbol for God in Its creative aspect. It is a symbol for God the *Creator*.

Symbols have power because they are patterns of creation. They show up everywhere, from the most sublime to the most mundane. The circle, for instance, is a universal form. We find it in the very smallest to the very largest scales in the cosmos. From atom to cell to planet to Solar System, the circle is there. But we must realize that the universal circular form isn't drawn; it is *created*. Any time we impact something with something else, we create shock waves that radiate outwards in all directions. We create a *circle*.

In Sanskrit, the word *anahata* means "not hit" or "the sound that is not made by the impact of two things." It refers to the sound of Spirit—the *Aum*—the Word of God. We are all familiar with physical sounds, the sound that *is* made when two things strike each other. The universal form of the circle is merely reflected in physical substance. It does not originate in matter. "My kingdom is not of this world," said Jesus. The symbol of the circle is of a higher order of reality. It is spiritual, not material. As priests, when we create a circle, we do so with our *being*, not with our fist.

When used as a symbol for God, the circle *without* a dot represents a field of undifferentiated creative power—pure potential. Right away we can see that the dot is the instigator of creative activity, the thing that brings undifferentiated power into specific manifestation. The symbol of the circle *with* a dot is therefore a universal symbol that describes the pattern by which *anything* is brought into being—from pure undifferentiated potential into a clear idea, which will subsequently be brought into manifested form.

How do we apply this knowledge to the Priesthood? One way is by seeing the altar top as a field of undifferentiated potential. Typically, altars are covered with white linen—a blank slate, as it were. Whatever we place upon the altar symbolizes the things we want God to bring into our lives. The bread and wine, at one level, symbolize food and drink: *give us this day our daily bread.* At another level, they symbolize our transformation by the infusion of Christ into our being.

The conscious use of symbols is a powerful tool. In spiritual terms, we perform our actions while being conscious of the creative power of God. We are in It, and It is within us—*I and the Father are one.* By performing our actions in this way, we get to feel the movement of God's energy (the Holy Spirit) move through us. But we do not merely *feel* it; we also get to intelligently *direct* it.

123

The Triangle

The triangle is truly an abstract symbol. It describes activity, not form. It is our intelligent use of the creative power of God. Always present in our life, it is as basic and fundamental as breathing. It is the principle of polarity in action. In its simplest sense, the triangle describes how we can create a need that God will fill. In an esoteric sense, it describes humanity's position between heaven and Earth—Creator, Mediator, Creation. It *is* the Holy Trinity.

The principle of the "trinity" shows up everywhere, especially in our technology-based modern world. Wherever there is positive and negative potential energy separated by a mediating substance, the trinity is in action. An electric battery, for example, is made of two elements (copper and zinc) separated by an electrolytic fluid that causes a chemical reaction between them. When the two poles are connected with a conductor, electricity flows.

This same principle shows up in the cells of our bodies. The fluids outside of the cell have a different potential energy than the fluids inside the cell. These are separated by an *intelligent* membrane that allows only the needed substances to pass through. Any time we see a mediator between two different states of existence, we are seeing the Holy Trinity in action.

This principle has been known for thousands of years. It is perhaps the most basic natural law, more basic than the laws of thermodynamics. But when it was first articulated, there was no scientific vocabulary with which to express it, so it was interpreted as religious truth. It was simply how God created the world. As mystics and spiritual scientists—*as priests*—we understand that God's laws operate in all domains and that

Earth and heaven are two ends of the same spectrum. So it's easy to find spiritual principles at work in science, as well as it is to find scientific principles at work in our spiritual life.

As an institution, science has laid claim to this triune principle, describing it in its own terms—cause, medium, effect. Religious institutions have also claimed it as its own, using their own jargon. But since we are dealing with a fundamental aspect of reality, one that doesn't necessarily have anything to do with either science or religion, I think it becomes necessary for us to start thinking outside of the institution.

In psychology, for example, our awareness falls into three distinct categories:

1. the world out there
2. the entity we call "me"
3. and the deeper part of us for which we have no name.

Taken together, they comprise our experience. We know that they aren't really separate. The world *out there* actually exists as a product of the way our senses interpret the vibrations that reach them. Our eyes don't see anything— they simply convey information to the visual cortex of our brain, which uses it to construct an image.

The "me" part of us is a composite made up of these stored images and the ideas we have about them. We use our interpretations to form an entity we call the ego, which is comprised of the content or the stored images and ideas that we take personally.

The deeper part of us is the unknown—a realm of possibilities and strange forces. We can feel it, but we can't see it. We can observe its effects in our lives, but we can't always see its cause-and-effect relationships. We call it different things, but every name we give it somehow fails to capture what it is.

This is a brief summary of us, one that anyone can relate to. It is our own personal Holy Trinity. Sure, there are other ways to look at the Holy Trinity—Beings too vast to comprehend; the great creative law of the universe; Father, Son, and Holy Spirit—but these are concepts. Let's bring it closer to home and let the theologians and metaphysicians argue about the rest. A good way to tell whether information of this kind is pertinent in *your* life is to ask yourself if it's something you can use *right now*.

Energy is constantly moving through these three aspects of us, aspects that seem to be separate but are actually three aspects of one thing. This is why the equilateral triangle has always been used to describe the Trinity—three essential components equal to each other. Take away any one of them and the triangle disappears. By working in threes, we gain an advantage over focusing on one aspect at a time, because in reality all activity, whether personal or cosmic, has this same tripart expression. When we look at manifestation, things take on a four-part structure. But we will go into that when we consider the third basic symbol, the square.

Understanding how our thoughts affect the world we see—and how the world we see affects our thoughts—enables us to understand *everything*. Add to that the deeper part of us—the unknown—and the entire mystery is revealed. But as Buddha said, "This cannot be taught."

And even Jesus said, "I am the *way*," which we can take to mean, "I am how you get there, not the destination itself." Becoming aware of our three seemingly separate aspects and sensing the energy that passes between them will lead us into a greater experience of God's reality, the God in Whom we live, move, and have our being.

The wind bloweth where it listeth, and thou hearest the sound thereof, but canst not tell whence it cometh, and whither it goeth: so is every one that is born of the Spirit. John 3:8

The Square

Whereas the energy of a circle is transformative, the energy of the square is stabilizing and consolidating. The circle acts like a conduit, allowing energy to move from one state to another; the square is a fixed system. The energy still moves, but is conservative, in that everything it does is for the purpose of conserving its present configuration.

In politics, for example, conservatives seek to preserve time-honored traditions, while liberals (or progressives) look for innovation and reform. (This is a very broad assessment not intended to spark debate.) Obviously, you can't have a viable system without both of these elements existing in dynamic balance with each other.

Another example is the human nervous system with its sympathetic and parasympathetic networks. One speeds up metabolism, and the other slows it down. Too much of either will kill us, but a dynamic balance between the two allows us to adapt to changing conditions. Adaptation is the hallmark of viability.

So the circle and the square act in polar opposition in the act of creation, not in conflict but in balance—a *dynamic* balance. When we omit one or favor one over the other, we get out of balance. If all we want in our spiritual life is to experience the flow of God's energy, that energy will eventually make it impossible for us to live in the world. On the other hand, if all we want is a belief structure with rules to follow, then the Spirit will wane, and we will become crystallized, not only spiritually but physically as well. The correct way to live is a middle path between these two, a path that meanders from side to side in a never-ending process of self-correction. In this way, we can evolve and at the same time *consolidate* the gains we make. It's a perfect system.

The square is by definition width and breadth. Within it we can plot out any image to any degree of resolution. In order to bring that image into manifestation, we have to consider how we turn the square into a cube. This involves time. Time exists for the purpose of creation. Genesis alludes to this by dividing the creative process into *days*. These are not literal days, of course, but cycles of any duration. The technical term is "periodicity." Time can only be understood within the context of eternity, which ironically has nothing to do with time. Time is merely a way to divide up that which is indivisible, an imposition of pattern onto a seamless whole. Periodicity—*In the beginning was the Word*.

Time involves sequence and repetition. These two aspects can be applied in whatever cycle you choose, whether a day, a year, a breath, or a heartbeat. The duration is unimportant, but the pattern is everything. Applying time, which includes sequence and repetition, to an image that is essentially two-dimensional (an image in the mind) is the basis of prayer and ritual. This is *how* it works. Then, with suitable preparation in the physical world, you get the bridge you need to bring your idea into reality.

Once the physical foundation has been laid, the creative fires start to burn, and the draft of that flame will draw the needed materials into the form. But there must be alignment between the form and the image. This is represented symbolically by the figure-eight (8 = 2 x 2 x 2, or 2 *cubed*). In Key 8 of the Tarot, we see a female figure, representing the subconscious mind, using a garland of flowers to harness the forces of nature. A garland is an orderly sequence, the repetition of a pattern woven over time. Such a pattern, when completed, is indestructible, which is another way of saying *eternal*. The gates of hell (chaos) shall not prevail against it.

Once a pattern such as this is established, it becomes a nexus in the mind—a *living* thing. It begins to breathe and grow. As it grows, it draws to itself all of the substance it requires for manifestation. It has to manifest, otherwise there would be an imbalance between the mind and the physical. Whatever exists in the mind MUST exist in the physical, and whatever exists in the physical MUST exist in the mind. This is the Law. If its existence is untenable, either in mind or the physical, the form will disintegrate.

Ritual and the Triangle

Ritual is pattern, and the triangle describes how patterns are made. There is only one drawing board—the Mind of God. Our minds are little roped-off partitions of it. And just as a piece of a hologram contains the complete pattern of the whole, so do our minds contain the entire structure of the Mind of God.

One of the biggest conundrums to ever come down theology's pike is this question: "If a priest, by virtue of the knowledge he or she has of Divine Law, can cause the power of God to manifest according to the pattern set by a ritual, then is the priest more powerful than God?" This question could only have been dreamed up by an egotist who had absolutely no understanding of either God or the Priesthood. Asking this question is the same as wondering whether cooking food with fire is an act of magic.

Science is science. It wasn't until the early 1800's that we knew of the existence of electromagnetism. When someone saw that a compass needle would deflect from magnetic north if it was brought close to a live electrical wire, two natural forces that had previously been thought to be unrelated were suddenly and irrevocably joined—two sides of the same coin—and the world changed forever. Modern technology became possible in that moment. And though it was a heady time for the scientific community, they knew that they hadn't invented electromagnetism but had merely discovered it. It had been there all along.

There are two reasons why I bring this up. One is to illustrate the power of understanding how nature works, the laws by which it operates and the impersonal nature of those laws. God sends the rain to fall on the just and the unjust alike. And two, to use this as a segue to the problem we have today, namely the belief that electromagnetism is the only useable kind of energy that we have to work with. (I know there is nuclear energy also, but so far all we use it for is warfare and the generation of *electricity*.) But there is another kind of energy—the energy of mind. And I don't mean the power of persuasion; we're not talking about communication between one person and the mob. We are talking about communicating with...

And here's the problem: If I say "the Mind of God" or I say "the mind of nature," neither would be entirely correct, because they are commonly regarded as separate things. If I say "the Mind of God," then we're back to a power struggle, as though we were trying to usurp God's power. If I say "the mind of nature," then we're talking about spells and incantations—*magic*. Only a deeply split personality could come up with a scenario like that—God against man, man against nature. The only thing that kind of thinking has produced is a bunch of corrupt priests making their living by taking protection money from superstitious believers. But in the final analysis there is only science. If there is a cause, there will be an effect. And what the Priesthood has known for millennia is that *mind is cause*.

So, why ritual? Why have an altar, why have candles, why have priests? If it's all happening in the mind, why do we *need* all of these external trappings? The truth is... we don't. The paraphernalia of ritual are there as *aids*, not agencies. But if we didn't have a physical *action*, could there be a physical result? Think about it—first we pray, and then we *act* according to our prayer. The prayer is answered *through* our action. Action is the agency of prayer, not things.

Whenever we contact the Mind of God, which is to say, whenever we connect with the All, power flows *immediately*. At that moment, we are the priest at the altar. By setting up a physical altar and sanctuary in such a way that it symbolizes the spiritual universe, and by physically and by convention separate it from the world as a sacred space, we set the stage for a narrative—we *say how it's going to go*. The power we are working with is every bit as real as electromagnetism, but the wires we are connecting are mental, not physical. The energy we are directing is spiritual, not electrical.

If you doubt the reality of this, consider how you use these principles every day in your life. Every time you transmute one emotion into another—such as anger into resolve—you are saying how it will go. By adaptation, you are re-creating the narrative. You are taking the one energy and telling it what to do, or rather how it's going to manifest in your body. You are a priest unto yourself. The priest at the altar is taking the energy of the One and adapting it to a specific need. He or she is standing in for the Whole Body of God. If the priest has the consciousness, she can say, "This is My Body," and in that moment speak as God. And because the patterns conform to universal patterns, the One energy will gladly cooperate.

All of this does not say that God is only energy. To read it that way is a mistake. But neither does it deny that there *is* energy in the Mind and Body of God. That which is above is as that which is below. We have a mind; we have a body. Our thoughts direct the energies of our body. We offer our mind and our body as a stand-in whenever we approach the altar, whether that altar is in a sanctuary or at the center of our being. Once we state our intention, we *swallow* it, just as we would swallow a morsel of food. And as that morsel descends into our core to become us, so does our intention become the energy that radiates outward into our world to transform it.

As long as you think of the triangle as lines on a piece of paper, you will not grasp the principle it stands for. At the same time, you cannot ignore the geometry of it. A circle is just a circle, but stand in the middle of one, and you can feel a shift in the energy. Your true north is suddenly redirected inward. The same applies to the triangle. Standing with one other person is different from standing with two other people. The energy is different—distinctly so. You have *this*, and you have *that*. And there you are, mediating between and *adapting* the two. This is the essence of the symbol of the Triangle.

CHAPTER 20

HEAD, HEART, AND WILL

Here's another way that you can look at your own personal *three-ness*:

- your head
- your heart
- your will

There are certainly other parts just as real, but these seem to form the main three. In working with our head, our heart, and our will, we naturally rise up out of our generative nature and begin to see ourselves as more than a body. We start to become aware of ourselves as energetic beings—spiritual, intellectual, and alive.

Normally, we approach the world with only one of these aspects, or at least we find that one is dominant. This forms a distorted triangle, a state of imbalance. For instance, if we are all mind, we become too analytical, and we get caught up in the many choices life has to offer. We are unable to choose among the many alternatives. If we are all heart, we lose the ability to discriminate or make distinctions. The world begins to blend together, not as a unified whole but as pool of interpenetrating awarenesses. This can be wonderful, but joy can quickly turn into sorrow, and sorrow into despair. The world seems to always be happening *to* us—not *because* of us. And if we are all willpower, we are great at getting things done, but it is usually at the expense of others. We become the hammer that sees everything as a nail. Instead of joining things together, we tend to break them apart. And though we are good at starting projects, rarely are we able to bring them to a meaningful conclusion.

So, achieving a balance of these three aspects brings a powerful harmony into our lives. How do we do this? Simply by focusing our awareness on them and then observing how the energy moves. We do this through the three activities of concentration, meditation, and contemplation—we learn to focus our awareness, we learn to be receptive to our higher nature, and we learn how to interact with what comes. These are the tools every priest should have in order to be an effective servant of God within the One Mind.

Training Your Will

Spiritual geometry begins with a dot—the center. It actually begins with the circle, but the dot is the first thing that manifests, so that's where we begin. After the dot comes the straight line. It is the radius of the manifested field that will follow. The straight line is the first outward movement, and it is the first thing to master after learning concentration.

Rather than try to explain what this is, here is an exercise that will *show* you, in terms of your own vehicle, what this primary symbol is all about.

- While sitting, place your hands just above your knees, about twelve inches apart with the palms facing each other.
- Look at them.
- Feel the blood coursing through them, and feel the energy in the nerves.
- See the energy as white light, as though the energy in the nerves of your hands and arms were lighting up, causing them to glow.
- Now, without physically moving your hands, bring them together. See the energy forms come together in front of you and clasp hands.
- You have just demonstrated the power of will with your spiritual body.

Work with this long enough, and you will be able to project energy wherever you want.

The reality is that this is how you move your physical body anyway. Your physical body moves as an effect of your spiritual body. As your spiritual body moves, your physical body moves. When you reach out your hand to pick up a glass of water, it is an idea in motion. It is the idea coupled with will that is the *real* action. The body, through the agency of your central nervous system, *responds* to the idea.

Take away the body, and the idea remains, and so does the action. But the action no longer takes place on the physical plane. Rather, it takes place on the spiritual plane, which is to say, the plane of *energy*. The action can no longer affect the glass of water, but it can affect the energy *within* the glass of water. Physical acts upon physical; energy acts upon energy.

In reality, the world of energy is much more real than the world of matter. Matter is, after all, congealed energy. Look at matter close enough, and there is nothing material about it. It is *all* energy. So learning to work with energy gives us a tremendous advantage when it comes to working with matter. The problem is that we never think to do it. Or if we do think of it, we somehow regard it as less real than the physical world.

The term "willpower" is misunderstood. Usually it means to suppress an impulse or to exert oneself towards a goal. Instead, consider it as *power*, which requires no effort and no exertion. All it requires is a yes or a no. Saying yes is like hooking up live wires to an electrical circuit. Once the contact is made, the power flows. It's not your power; you did nothing to cause the flow of energy except make the connection. The energy flows *because* of you; it doesn't flow *from* you. You are the channel of power, not its source. Likewise, saying no is simply breaking the connection.

Training Your Mind

How do we make and/or break a connection? We do it by either associating or disassociating ideas in our mind. For example, by associating a basketball with the action of it sailing through the air and through the hoop, we tell the story of what's going to happen. Similarly, if we lay our hands on a person's head and visualize them as healthy, we associate the idea of blessing with the idea of healing. We set a pattern for how the energy will flow. The decision to make this association is the act of saying "yes." Conversely, if we see something that we want to go away, we erase the idea of it from our mind and immediately replace it with its opposite. "What we bind on Earth, we bind in heaven; what we loose on Earth, we loose in heaven."

Another easy application of this principle is in blessing our food. We cannot change the physical composition of food, but we can greatly alter the vital energies within it. This has obvious benefits for our physical health, since the body utilizes the energies within food much more than it does the gross substance. But *in reality*, chemistry is nothing but energy, so don't let your disbeliefs or your opinions get in the way of changing what can be changed.

Simply visualizing the energy in your hands is not enough when it comes to actually *working* with energy. You have to learn how to project it. This is where the "straight line" of the dot at the center of the circle comes in. The straight line is a visible representation of using your will. No effort is involved; this happens strictly within your consciousness. Volition requires no force, because volition IS force. It is always in action, although we aren't usually aware of it. All we have to do is think about it, and energy flows. We don't have to yell at it. All we have to do is to see the completed action and then say "yes."

This is subtle work. There is very little fanfare, few special effects. But then, what's more important, making a show of it or getting the job done? The trick is to let IT do the work. Mind (with a capital M) is a powerful thing—the *most* powerful thing in the universe. And it is completely at our disposal. In fact, it is *happy* to fulfill our every desire. This is, after all, the way that you do everything that you do. As a priest, you need to learn to do it consciously.

Doing the exercise with your hands shows you that you can use your energy independently of your body, which will come in handy after you leave your physical vehicle behind at the end of this lifetime. Of course, there are endless ways you can use this *before* you die. The fun part is exploring the opportunities on your own, perhaps with a few helpful hints along the way.

Training Your Heart

We can only want what we value. Take away the value, and you take away the desire. If you want something that you *think* is valueless, or worse yet, harmful, then there is a component of value in it that you are unaware of. Your job is to find out what it is.

Training your heart involves studying your desires. If you want something that's not good for you, then somewhere in your mental circuitry you have made a false connection. You have associated two ideas that are incompatible. The act of smoking, for example, can be wrongly associated with feeling important—someone who should be taken seriously. The desire of wanting to feel important, as though your life matters, is real. It's the association of that desire with the act of smoking that's not. That association was engineered by those who sell cigarettes. Once you realize that the association is unreal, you can then set about addressing the actual desire—the need to have your life matter. That can lead to all kinds of exciting possibilities. But if you substitute those possibilities with the act of smoking, you effectively keep them from materializing. Then your life potential runs the risk of going up in smoke.

The worst thing you can do to your heart is to deny that your desires are legitimate. This is absolutely forbidden. When the mind and the will gang up on the heart like this, all kinds of health problems can arise. Rather than condemn your desires, investigate the associations that underlie them. It's a wiring problem, not a moral one.

Study your desires. Find out what's at the root of them. But don't do it as an inquisitor; do it with love. They are *your* desires after all. Coax them, woo them, find out what they really want. It's almost always not what they act out. They only do that out of rebellion—they will not be denied! But with love, they stop their self-destructive behavior, and their inner beauty shines through. The more you acknowledge their innocence, the faster they will reveal it to you.

Putting the Three Together

Let's go back to the circle with a dot in the center. Now that you know what this symbol business is really about, let's look at it again.

You know that concentration is the ability to hold your attention on a single idea (or object) for an extended period of time without letting your mind wander to an unrelated thought. Fine. But what if you concentrate *without* an idea or an object? In other words, what if you gather in all of your energy—you know, the stuff you normally let bleed out into the world. What if you gather all of that into the center of you, that place where you actually reside? You know from the above exercise what we're talking about when we say "energy." Now you're going to concentrate all of it into a single dot, not through exertion but *by seeing it there.*

You will find that when you do this that the field around you (the circle) gets emptied out. There is nothing in it. But here's the rub: *nature abhors a vacuum.* So unless you establish a boundary to your field of nothingness, a lot of "stuff" is going to rush in to fill it. So, the trick (or skill) is to both establish the center and simultaneously hold the boundary.

This requires coordinating your mind and your will. But the outcome, what determines the *quality* of the energies that fill in the vacuum you create, is wholly up to your heart, your desire, your *longing.* What do you long for? This is the most important question anyone can ever ask. Many people go through their entire life protecting themselves from knowing what that is. Why would they do such a thing? Because they believe in the false associations between their desires and the alleged objects of their desires. The false associations are like scary masks—*demons' masks.* But when we look for the desire behind the mask, the mask comes off, and we discover what makes us feel alive!

The best way to find out what your longing is—what it is that you really want—is to ask yourself, "What do I *love?*" This works much better than asking what it is you *want.* Most wants are superficial anyway. But what you love comes from the core of your soul. In the Book of Revelation, the angel says, "Nevertheless I have somewhat against thee, because thou hast left thy first love." Get back to *that!*

Visualization

Don't worry if you're not a "visual" person. Visualization is a learned skill, and it can be learned very easily. Here's a brief description of an exercise that will have you visualizing in no time: Place a lighted candle in front of you in a dark room. Examine every aspect of it—the light, the wax, the flame, the process of combustion. After you have done this and it occupies your entire awareness, extinguish the flame, close your eyes, and see the candle in your mind. Simple, huh? This will develop your ability to visualize very quickly.

The important thing is to *work with this!* Every time you get in your car, see yourself arriving at your destination. Every time someone tells you they're sick, see them healthy. Every time you put a key into a lock, see the door opening before you push on it. This is learning to use your will. Until and unless you learn this, you can have all the good intentions in the world and still be ineffective. You can be as gentle as a dove and not know how energy works.

Give it a shot. Experiment with this and record your observations. Be methodical but also inventive. Remember that energy is real and that there *will* be results. So...be gentle.

Chapter 21

Inner Guidance

Inner guidance comes in many forms. Some people hear a distinct message, some have visions, some find themselves caught up in the spirit of the moment, and the right thing to do spreads out before them like a roadmap. We are each born with certain spiritual gifts—some with more, some with less, some unique and specific, some general and broad. Some have the ability to heal, others the ability to teach, and some have the ability to be a friend to all of humanity.

Have you ever considered that your spiritual gift *is* your guidance? In the parable of the Ten Talents, a man getting ready to go on a trip gives each of his employees a different amount of money and tells them to go out and put it to work. He doesn't take them by the hand and tell them what to do at every turn. He just says to go out and make it grow.

The point of the story is clear: use what you've been given. Make the most of what you're good at.

If your talent is healing, heal. If it's teaching, teach. If your talent is love, go out and spread love. Doesn't it make sense that *that* is your guidance? The particulars of your mission don't really matter. That's the human mind talking. The overall plan, however, matters a lot! Because, at some point, when all is said and done, someone's going to ask you, *"Whadaya got?"*

We don't have to wait for inner auditory messages, necessarily. They can be hard to verify. Too many of them can make us figuratively (and sometimes literally) crazy. Neither are "signs" any more reliable. Look for them too often, and soon that's all you will see. But when they come, especially when they come unbidden, pay attention. Oftentimes, they are your higher intelligence trying to make you aware of hidden connections. Just as it would be foolish to ignore what's right in front of your eyes, so too is it foolish to ignore your intuition.

But it's always wise to remember that we see what we want to see and hear what we want to hear, which is why renunciation is so important in the life of a priest. We can get so focused on a goal that the universe cannot help but reflect it to us everywhere. That doesn't mean that what we're seeking is right; it just means that we're the ones making it happen, not God. Jesus said that *whatsoever* we ask for will be given. This is the Law of Prayer in action. Unless we can back away from our zeal from time to time and empty our pockets, so to speak, at the feet of the Almighty, we run the risk of becoming willful. And being willful is different from having a strong will. We can *use* a strong will, but willfulness always uses us.

In life, we do the things we have to do, the things we are *driven* to do. Our desires run like water down the side of a mountain. It's the fire in our lives that tempers the torrent. Fire is the demands life places upon us. As we respond to those demands, our desires get purified. They get focused. We are forged in the furnace of our needs. Desire shapes the steel; necessity hardens it so that it can hold an edge. Never resent the necessities in your life. They are God's gift to you.

Our spiritual gifts are the outgrowth of that which we love—we must be true to them. As we devote ourselves to the things we love, guidance comes easily and freely. Therefore, if you ever feel stuck, remember your first love. "Follow your bliss," as Joseph Campbell said. This is the true "rapture"—love always lifts us up out of the world. And from that higher vantage point, it's much easier to see which way to go.

CHAPTER 22

DEATH AND RESURRECTION

The life of a professional minister is not easy. You don't always get to go where you want, and you certainly don't get to pick your congregation or your board of directors. Oftentimes, you can find yourself in a church that feels foreign or even strange. You ask yourself, "What am I doing here?" But faith gives you the strength to stay, knowing (or hoping) that God will lead the way.

There are two approaches that you can take in a situation like this. You can either set about trying to move your people to where you think they should be, spiritually speaking, or you can—like the seed that must be buried and die before it can bear fruit—allow yourself to be subsumed by your congregation, surrendering yourself to its collective mind, knowing that God will raise you up again. And as it is said that Jesus raised the whole planet with him when he rose from the dead, so will you raise the consciousness of your congregation when you resurrect yourself from the invisible forces of their collective understanding.

The trick here is that you must *become* them before you can save them. This is the essence of the teaching of the Incarnation—the Word became flesh. You must take on the "flesh" of their collective mind and make it your own, knowing that it isn't your *ideas* that are going to change them, but the Spirit of God moving through you. Death comes in many forms, and dying to your perceived self in order to take on the collective mind of your church is a form of dying. You not only must know your audience, you must become one of them. To be a "fisher of men," you have to offer yourself as both bait and hook. You will be swallowed whole. The deeper the fish takes the hook into its belly, the better able you will be to lift it into your boat.

How is this done? You know the saying: if you want people to accept you, listen more and talk less. Show them that you are interested in them; let them know that you care about them; and by all means, let them know that they can *trust* you. In short, love them. Don't try to teach them until you have gained their trust. If you jump the gun on this, they will fight you tooth and nail. Besides, the best way to get an idea to stick is to present it in such a way that they think it was theirs all along. Let them take the credit.

What I'm describing here is different from "go along to get along." I'm not saying that you have to kowtow to anyone's ego or roll over to opportunistic demands from your board. They will try to make changes that they couldn't get past the previous minister. You can listen to their concerns without committing to anything. Let them know that you are willing to work with them, but stay detached—friendly, but detached.

But this is nothing new, nor is it especially spiritual. Any book on management can give you plenty of advice on how to adapt in your new position. So, you are going to have to rely on your spiritual abilities, if you are to make the changes you want to see in your new church. While you are busy "dying," like the seed that you are, you must also be sowing the seeds that you want to see come to fruition sometime down the road. You're playing the long game. And the way you do that is to become conscious of who you are on the spiritual level, the power and the energy that you are bringing into the collective mind of your congregation.

None of us can simply change who we really are, the baggage we carry with us, or the intentions of our hearts—the ones we have cultivated over a lifetime. These things cannot die, not even temporarily. But what we can do is keep them in the background. Do not assert them, at least not until you have gained the trust of your people. In the meantime, let the unspoken part of you do the heavy lifting. Let the "body" of your soul do the work of planting the energetic seeds, the feeling, the spiritual orientation that you have developed throughout your life. Do your spiritual work at night—your meditations, your devotions, your prayers—and let it follow you around during the day, silently and effectively. *But do not say anything about it.* The moment you talk about it, the energy gets diverted, and your presence devolves into an opportunity for debate. Every time you debate someone, whether it's religion or politics or church policies, you erode trust. Always bring the focus back to *them*, and as you do, they will open up. That's when the invisible presence you're carrying around will find its way into their hearts.

As long as your intentions are pure, and as long as you are keeping up with your own spiritual work, the presence you carry will be imbued with the presence of God. So you don't have to worry whether they're getting the real thing. Of course, there will always be those who think that it's "you," that it's your personality, your *soul*, or your physical presence that they're feeling. But that's easy enough to deflect (and you had better deflect it!) by bringing the attention back to them and their relationship with God. Always pass the glory up to God; never accept it for yourself. You don't have to be obnoxious about it by correcting people every time they compliment you; just *do* it by redirecting their attention to what's real. They will get the message, either consciously or subconsciously.

Pastoral work is subtle, more subtle than most people realize. If all you're there for is to teach the Bible, you might as well be that—a Bible teacher. But if you're there to get people into heaven, you have got to know your stuff. You have to know how to work *spiritually*.

It's the outer you that dies when you take up your position with a new congregation, but it's the *inner* you that comes to life. This is the resurrection. This is how you lead people to God. You have to be there, and then they will come to you. But they won't if you're constantly preaching at them.

So keep your personality, your charisma, and your charm in check, but especially your *knowledge*. Dial them way back. If some of your members want knowledge, and that's all they want, send them to Barnes and Noble. If it's charisma and charm they're looking for, send them to a New Age seminar. But keep your spiritual presence intact.

This book is for priests, regardless of what profession you're in. And if you happen to be a priest who is also a minister, then this chapter will help you straddle that fence. Just remember that there are plenty of ministers in the world already. If some of your people are looking for that kind of pastoral performance, maybe you should hire one. Or maybe they should find another church. Either way, keep your spiritual work first, and everything else will be added unto you.

PART 4

YOUR MISSION—
SHOULD YOU
CHOOSE TO
ACCEPT IT

CHAPTER 23

THE BUCK STOPS HERE

I once had a picture of a South American peasant herding goats along a barren mountain path. It seemed to capture the spirit of what it means to be a priest. The peasant was wearing a red cloak over a white tunic, reminiscent of so many pictures of our high priest, the Good Shepherd. And while it might seem arrogant to equate a pastor's flock with a herd of animals, it nonetheless accurately describes what a priest does. He or she takes people from where they are to where they could be. They take them from the squalid lowlands of self-indulgence to the rarified heights of spiritual attainment.

The Priesthood is responsible for the spiritual well-being of humanity. Sounds like an exaggeration, does it not? Nevertheless, it's true. When we become priests, we are given tools that we could never have developed on our own.

We get connected into a network that is of heaven, not of Earth. We are the agency of that network that makes Earth's connection with heaven possible. We are the functional part of the mediation of Christ Jesus—it happens *through* us. This doesn't mean that Christianity is the only true religion or that everyone has to "confess the Lord." The name "Jesus" is certainly powerful, but the Spirit of the Christ, regardless of what name we give it, is the real power. The life energy of this Solar System is a holy thing, an aspect of God. It is intelligent and imbued with love. It is that which we mediate. It is a *spiritual reality*, not a belief system.

The traditional party line of Christianity is that it is the One True Religion and Jesus Christ the *only* Son of God. Whether or not we take the stories of Jesus literally as they are given in the New Testament, it is imperative that we also understand that these stories are told in *symbolic language*. The "cross" that Jesus said we must carry is *not* a literal cross. The path we are to follow is not a literal path. Our death on the cross is not a physical death. The Way is a *living* Way devised by a living God for the purpose of waking us up and making us more alive—*not dead!*

There are three things that we must *know* if we are to have any effect on the spiritual well-being of the world:

1. We have to know that we are one with the whole human race. There is no fundamental separation between an individual and the whole of humanity. We share the same mind and the same body (all human bodies are fundamentally the same), and we all do pretty much the same things. Even if we don't kill people with guns, we kill them with our

thoughts. Anger, hatred, and violence, as well as love, kindness, and compassion, are fundamental commonalities to us all.

2. We have to know that we have absolute control over our own inner life, that we choose the thoughts we think, and that we have the ability to channel our emotional energies in positive ways. No one can force us to think the way they think; we have to agree to it. Believing that you are subject to preconditioning assures that you will be. And, having a bad experience doesn't mean you have to respond to it the way everyone else does—you can choose to respond *differently*.

3. We have to know that our thoughts and actions have *power*, that our words and deeds can move mountains. It's not that we are personally powerful, but as we align ourselves with right action, both internally and externally, we open up a channel between Earth and heaven. Through that channel pours the grace of God, empowering everything we say and do. Our life becomes a sacrament—a *living sacrifice*—and a high road that others can follow.

This is how we take responsibility for the spiritual health of the world. Simultaneously, we know that everything happens within us—we don't have to stand on a soapbox and scream at the crowd. What we do to ourselves affects *everyone*; our apparent separation from each other is an illusion.

Priests have authority over themselves. It is only by their connection with the whole of humanity that they have authority over others. As they align themselves with God, God's grace flows through them, affecting everyone and everything around them. However, when people are asleep, spiritually speaking, when they have surrendered themselves to the forces of nature, to external causes, with no understanding of the Law of Cause and effect or the power of their thinking, they are like boats without rudders—they will drift whichever way the current takes them. Priests are the gatekeepers. They determine which way the waters will flow—not by their own power, but by the way they live their lives, by the way they use their Word, by the thoughts they allow themselves to think, and by the spiritual values they hold in their hearts. When others have abnegated their personal responsibility for their own destinies, it falls to those who are conscious of the Laws of Creation to help them. It is a responsibility we do not want to shirk: "But woe unto you, scribes and Pharisees, hypocrites! For ye shut up the kingdom of heaven against men: for ye neither go in yourselves, neither suffer ye them that are entering to go in." To stand by and do nothing when the whole world is crying out for action is a sin against the Spirit.

Spiritual self-responsibility is the cross that priests must bear. No matter who we are, priest or not, no one can do our spiritual work for us. We cannot advance spiritually on the coattails of another person, not even our spiritual teacher. We each stand alone before our creator, and we are each responsible for our responses to life. No one can dictate that to us unless we let them.

There is only One Person, the blueprint of which is a kind of broadcast that we all tune into, our flesh and our thoughts struggling to attune themselves with it. It's the broadcast that's real, that stream of intelligence coming from God. Our individual minds and bodies are our soul's attempt to learn from and align with *that*. Somehow, we have all clustered around this divine signal—*the Son of God*—captured by its extraordinary beauty, and have committed ourselves to realizing its perfection.

But people are human, and they will seek their divine image each in their own way and at their own pace. Accepting this as a fundamental part of human nature frees us up to see the broadcast—the *God* in them. It is the broadcast we love, the power of God that flows through their soul, not the outer personality. As we give it our attention, the signal grows stronger. This is what priests do.

Taking responsibility for the entire human race is impossible without honesty. You have to be really clear about human frailty, both in others and in yourself, before you can see past it to the God Being within each person. Our responsibility is to give life to the broadcast, not to fix human nature. Human nature will change in time through its exposure and its surrender to the signal radiating outward from its soul, not by the rules you impose. External enforcement has its place in human affairs, but without this dedication to serving the *real* person, rules and regulations will kill a person›s spirit. Why? Because people can always tell when the rules exist solely for the benefit of the rule-makers. And that is an affront to the Divine Spirit within each and every human being.

It takes a lot of discipline to see past human nature to the pure, clear broadcast from the Mind of God that each human soul is trying, in its own way, to emulate. As priests, our job is to provide a zone of compassion where a soul can feel safe enough to explore its attraction to the Divine. This is how we take responsibility for the spiritual well-being of the human race.

Now, look in the mirror and say, "The buck stops here."

CHAPTER 24

SEEING EARTH AND HEAVEN TOGETHER

As we interact with our fellow human beings, it's *how* we see them that makes a difference. And the best thing we can do for people is to see them in such a way that makes their journey towards soul-development easier, safer, and faster. We do this by seeing their connection to the ever-present, all-pervasive Life of God.

In mystical language, this process is called the "path of initiation." In Christian mysticism, it is called "The Way." It is the process of identification with the One Life. Since all people are fundamentally the same, both physically and spiritually, the Way is the same for everyone—one life energy, one humanity, one Way. Unfortunately, the literalists of all religions (but especially Christianity) take this general principle and turn it into a political platform, as in "Jesus is the *only* Son of God." What this means esoterically, however, is that union with the Divine can *only* come about by identifying ourselves with the One Life of God. And since all life in this Solar System has its origin in the Sun, it is only through the *power of life* that we can realize God, not by having better ideas about it.

Identification with the One Life comes in two stages: First, we look at nature and recognize that one force drives it. We see that that force comes from the Sun and that the multitude of life forms is an expression of the full spectrum of sunlight, the visible and invisible parts of it. Second, we come to see that the same force that drives nature drives our own body. This recognition sometimes emerges in our awareness with such force that it produces an experience of bright light in our inner vision. Our body fills with light, and we feel reborn. This experience is called the Illumination and is a significant milestone on the path of initiation.

Once we have become acclimatized to this new energy in our body, we see ourselves as an extension of the Sun, both figuratively and literally. We begin to realize that the Sun is everywhere, that we are *in* the Sun and not merely receiving its rays from a distance. This is literally true, because the entire Solar System is filled with the Solar radiation, the central Sun of which is merely its focal point. When we are in tune with the One Life, we see God everywhere.

As this idea takes root, a fundamental shift takes place in our awareness. It happens suddenly and without warning. What was once an external reality suddenly becomes *us*. We become aware of what has been true all along, that we *are* the Solar System and that its central focal point is mirrored in us. In religious terms, we become "one with

God." In the language of spiritual initiation, this is called "Self-realization." With our inner vision, we see God's focal point reflected in us at the center of our being, and we come to realize that we are a Son/Sun of God.

This central focal point is our true self, called the "Self," spelled with a capital "S" in order to differentiate it from our normal self, the one we regard as a separate entity in the world. The Self is the "image and likeness of God" in which we were created.

We realize that the source of the light we see within us—the light of life made visible in the Illumination—is this thing at the center of us. The center of our being ceases to be in our head. Our mind and our thoughts become peripheral to this emanation of conscious intelligence that streams forth from the center of our spiritual body.

It's at this point that nature begins to reveal its secrets, and inspiration and insight become our normal state of consciousness. Everywhere we look, something is revealed. Our former personality begins to fall away, and we become a new person altogether. We emerge into a higher order of being. New experiences come to us, and the entire world starts to look different.

The reality of the interconnectedness of life ceases to be an idea and instead becomes part of our everyday experience. The intelligence of the One Life starts spilling into our awareness, and we begin to experience it as a tangible reality. More and more, we start to know what it knows.

Its intelligence doesn't always occur to us in the language of our workaday life. Usually, it emerges from our depths as an unspecified knowing, an experience that we can't quite name. But then the external world starts to show evidence of it, revealing patterns or directing us to someone who can help us find what we need. It doesn't do this because we're special; it does it because the One Life is always seeking an opportunity—*any* opportunity—to harmonize with itself.

We begin to trust this new source of guidance, and we start to use it for everything, from the most mundane purposes to the most exalted spiritual insights. It grows and grows, and like John the Baptist, we say to ourselves, "I must decrease so that He may increase." We take on the Mind of Christ.

This power of God, which manifests as the focal point of our Solar System, gradually supplants all of the lies our limited senses have told us. And, it replaces them with a living, breathing connection with *everything*.

The experience of Self-realization is the core of the Priesthood. It is what gives it its authority. It is the manifestation of the interface, the direct connection with the Mind of God, the Christ in us. Without it, there is only head-knowledge and speculation, nothing but ideas and a dogged adherence to them. Such ideas can seem translucent to the mind and yet be opaque to the Spirit. When this happens, the light of life grows dim, and the world is deprived of grace as the Sun slips behind a cloud of reflexive ruminations.

Light is the power of life made visible. The two are inseparable. We only see a small part of the Sun's spectrum; the rest fills the space in which we live and energizes every cell in our body. The Sun is the Prime Mover (in terms of vibration) of the seen and unseen worlds. And, within its vibrations lies the intelligence—the *code*—that informs every particle of matter in our Solar System. It would be incorrect to say that the Sun *is* God, but it's entirely accurate to say that the Sun is the first manifestation of God. In the beginning was the Sun, and by the Sun all things were made.

Science tells us that we are literally made from the dust of stars, that the atoms in our bodies originated in the stars of our galaxy. All matter was "born" in these fiery furnaces so familiar to us in the nighttime sky. Each atom within us is a miniature solar system composed entirely of energy. We live in the midst of that energy—we live in the vibration of the stars.

The Ancients saw fire as a portal into higher worlds. They sensed that fire releases the energy of which matter is composed, and that this energy, when followed, would lead them into the unseen realms. Quaint language by today's standards, but the principle stands true—reality exists on many planes, most of which are beyond our ability to perceive. But rather than lose ourselves in the glamor of endless existence, let's simply tune into the energy right in front of our eyes. And, by "eyes," I mean our inner eyes as well, our inner vision that lets us look past the veil of matter into the eternal world of Spirit energy.

Why do we attach the word "Spirit" to the word "energy"? Because, energy by itself is lifeless and mechanical—just like electricity—whereas Spirit is intelligent and *alive*. Spirit is radiant. It radiates outwardly in all directions from each point of its manifestation. We live in a sea of its radiance. We are it, and it is us. Its mode of expression is *action*, and everywhere we see action, we are looking at Spirit. Just as there is no such thing as empty space, there is no place where Spirit does not express itself. After all, what else is there? In order for a thing to exist, it must be in a manifested form. Otherwise, it exists only as a nameless potential. Once named, it comes into being.

Are there states of existence beyond that of action and manifestation? Sure there are. *Brahma* of Hinduism and *The Father* of Christianity come before everything we know. They are unfathomable to the human mind. But the way to the ineffable is through the Word—the primary vibration of the cosmos in which we live. That vibration is all that exists in this world, and its permutations are the forms out of which all things are made.

To be a World Priest, you must function from the Word—not the "Word" of Christianity, not the historical personality of Jesus of Nazareth, but the Word with which Jesus of Nazareth identified himself, the Word that entered into him at the Baptism by John, the *Word of God*, the Firstborn of the Father, that point of emergence where the ineffable takes on form, having within itself the wholeness of the Being from which it comes.

This is the Word we must learn to embody, to use it as the carrier wave of the words we speak, the inner knowing with which we interact with the world. And the first step in realizing this Word is the Illumination—experiencing the light of Christ within our body. When we see that the life in us is the same life that expresses itself in nature, "the same force that through the green fuse drives the flower," recognizing that it's like a river that has its source high up in the mountains of Spirit, then we will see it within ourselves as the light that lights everyone, the Light of the World—*the Light of Christ.*

There is a protocol to follow on the spiritual path—new wine cannot be put into old bottles. You must first become aware of the living being of Christ, the primary vibration of the cosmos, and then let it work on you a little bit at a time, so that the increase in current doesn't cause your circuit breakers to pop. Many people have had their eyes opened to this reality before they were ready, and it made them feel like they were losing their minds. I know one person who experienced the light as a child. It scared her so badly that she has shunned it ever since.

Many churches characterize this experience as Satanic—ironic, to say the least. It keeps people afraid and perpetuates their dependence on external guidance. And guidance is the issue here. Once you become conscious of the energy of life, its currents and its intelligence are revealed to you. Your intuition comes alive. You know the difference between right and wrong, because the energy of life shows you. If a thing is right, energy flows, and a connection is made; if it's wrong, it doesn't work. But when something is right, it works for everyone, not just you. That's the nature of God's Spirit.

The spiritual path is fraught with danger for those who try to go it alone. This is why the institutionalized churches prohibit dabbling in the occult. What is the "occult"? It is the original "third rail," a metaphor referring to the third rail of an electrically powered train. Well, the occult is the third rail of religion, and not without good reason. Touch it, and it can kill you, spiritually speaking. The only problem with this is that occult phenomena are happening anyway —spontaneously—with or without preparation, so we have to talk about it. Otherwise, people will think that they are going insane.

There are many references in the Bible to the Illumination, but as always, they are couched in symbolic language. The parting of the Red Sea, Moses raising the serpent in the wilderness, the Baptism of John, and the Transfiguration on the Mount—all of these are stories about the Illumination and how to attain it. The most obvious of them is the raising of the serpent, a direct reference to Kundalini Yoga and a precursor to the Crucifixion. Why the Crucifixion? Sufi master, Hazrat Inayat Khan put it like this: *"It always means that you must sacrifice something very dear to you when God's call comes."*

The Illumination

So, let's get down to the mechanics of this thing called "Illumination," because it is a real experience with real effects. First, we have to recognize that in order to see light in one's body, there has to be a pathway for that to occur. This pathway is the nervous system. This should come as no surprise, seeing as how the nerves are the conductors of power, force, and energy—the interface between Earth and heaven. And this is really all we need to know in order to experience light. If you want to *understand* the process, that's a different matter, one that is best pursued *after* one has had the experience.

Normally, we tend to think that the "I," the *self*, resides in our head, somewhere behind the forehead. This is not true. What we perceive as the seat of consciousness is merely the reflection of a deeper center. If you look at the drawings of the old alchemists, you will see the moon at the head and the sun in the abdomen. The moon reflects the light of the sun, does it not? The pictures of the world we see are more like those on a movie screen than a direct perception. It stands to reason that we can learn more about the nature of reality by examining the projector than we can by analyzing the screen.

Here is a method by which you can locate the center of your being, which is essential if you want to find the source of light, the "central sun" of your personal solar system.

- First, close your eyes. Get quiet and become aware of your body's sense of itself in its immediate space. This is similar to doing any visualization exercise, but instead of constructing an image in your head, you are *sensing* something that is already there.
- Next, become aware of the space in front of you. (You don't have to project a line as in the previous exercise, just feel the space.) Feel the body's awareness of what's in front. Then, feel what's behind you. Project your awareness there—reach out with it.
- Then, do the same with the space to the left of you and the space to the right of you.
- Next, do the same thing with the space above you and the space below you.

If you have done these steps experientially and not with your intellect, if you *felt* the space and not merely thought about it or tried to see it with your visual sense, you will now feel the place out of which your awareness has sprung, the place from which it extends itself in these different directions. That place is in the center of your abdomen.

From here on out, this is your *true north*. This is your altar, your place of worship, your Holy of Holies. If you look at it with your mind's eye, it may appear rather solid, like a rock. But what looks like a surface is actually the "veil of matter." Underneath that surface is the Self of God—the real You—the *source* of all light in your being, not merely its reflection. Behind that veil is a light more brilliant than the noonday sun. And though you might not be able to see it yet, you can most definitely *feel* it. Light, after all, is light, whether you can see it or not. You can't see the electricity in the third rail of a subway track, but you know it's there!

This is the first step in having the experience called the Illumination. It is your natural state, something that has been there all along. It doesn't take a lot of effort on your part, only the desire to see it and the willingness to let go of preconceived ideas of who and *what* you are. Once you train yourself to habitually feel the center of your being, you will never again mistake your Self with the thoughts that rattle around in your brain.

The Priesthood is much more than the traditional roles assigned to it by society. We are the hierophants, the temple masters who shepherd souls through the paths of initiation. But before we can do that, we must be thoroughly grounded in those experiences ourselves. Fortunately, in this day and age, this is fairly easy, easier than it was in ancient times. The ambient energy available to us now is far greater than it was then, so much so that some people are entering into these experiences spontaneously. So we need to be ready to help them when they come to us for guidance. And we need to be able to help those who are seeking these experiences, those who are seeking the *reality* of God in their lives.

CHAPTER 25

THE NEW TEACHER-STUDENT RELATIONSHIP

It stands to reason that the Age of Aquarius would bring changes in all areas of life, including the time-honored traditions of the teacher/student relationship, perhaps especially in this area, since Aquarius represents a major course-correction in all things authoritative. Yes, authority is the issue. Specifically, it is the usurpation of it by any person who takes on the authority of God as if it were his own. Sure, you have to step into those shoes if you want to be effective in the world. But if and when (because all priests do this at some point in their career) you forget that it is God's authority and not yours, you will become, and I mean this in all sincerity, an insufferable pain in the ass.

Here is the essential truth about the teacher/student relationship: *teachers learn from their students.*

Now, if this seems like something you knew already, well...of course you knew it already. But what you may not have known is that the student doesn't know it, not usually. And this is where the playing field is changing. Every teacher/student relationship in the past has been based on the contract of *I will teach, and you will learn*. This is straightforward enough, and every teacher has taken comfort in its simplicity. The problem is that it's an entirely top-down affair. It is hierarchical and linear, with no room for feedback or the viability of a living system that feedback provides. The new contract, which both parties must enter into with eyes wide open, is *we will learn together*.

This is going to rankle the hell out of a lot of people, not only teachers, but students too. Why? Because it flies in the face of tradition. Why fix something that isn't broken? Well, guess what...it *is* broken. Every teacher who has set himself up as the ultimate authority in a student's life has only created more issues that the student will eventually have to work through, not unlike the issues they have with their parents.

The problem with this is that if you see your student as a *child*, he will behave like a child. He will abandon every shred of common sense that he has learned in his life, prior to meeting you, in order to fit your preconception of him. Instead of getting what he needs in order to live an independent spiritual life, which is *ostensibly* what you are trying to give him, he will adopt your idiosyncrasies, which for him are inappropriate. Why corrupt the good stuff with *your* stuff? Why inflict that on him?

Here's why this has become an issue. The Age of Aquarius is bringing in a new level of energy. Spiritual growth is happening faster and more spontaneously. In the words of the prophet, "No man will have to teach his neighbor, saying here is God, for all shall know me from the least to the greatest." Our task now is to help students cope with what they are experiencing *already.* God is becoming part of the landscape, as bright as the noonday Sun. And most people don't need to be told about the Sun, do they? They already know. Your job is to help them *deal* with it.

So, this is it. This is the new program. It doesn't invalidate what you know, neither does it put the student up on a pedestal. It makes the relationship *real.* We have always learned from our students, and we always will. Why try to keep that a secret? Deep down, the student knows it anyway. If we hide behind our robes and our rank, all we do is teach him how to pretend. After all, we are not in the business of creating clones. We want to help our students reveal *themselves,* not mimic us. Thinking that we already know who they are can only lead to cloning. If we think our spiritual sight is that good, we're kidding ourselves. It's not. Only God knows the true potential of each living soul. Teaching is a process of revelation—for *everyone* involved.

CHAPTER 26

THE INNER WORK

Our job as priests is to take ownership of the collective mind. As a body, this is the function of the Priesthood, the reason why it was instituted by those above. This means that above all else we must learn to control our thinking. And along with that, we must learn to exercise our will. Because unless we can breathe life into our ideas and speak them into manifestation, we cannot affect the world.

Speaking the Word of Power goes beyond merely having conviction. With conviction, we can persuade an audience of our ideas, but if our ideas are disconnected from reality, they can only live for a short time. People might adopt them, but they will adopt them in the same way they adopt a fad. Such ideas sustain themselves by contrast only, not through substance. In order for an idea to really live, it must correlate with an idea in the mind of God. When this happens, the alignment turns into a channel—the higher floods into the lower. When the intangible idea is brought into manifestation through the spoken word, real power moves, and its effect is unstoppable.

Today however, we have an interesting development, namely the rise of communications technology, wherein it is possible to float unsustainable ideas for greatly extended periods of time. This is done by shifting the public conversation away from print and into images. Images that are either taken out of context or are inappropriately coupled with strong emotion have taken the place of rational thought. If an emotionally provocative picture is presented often enough, and it is presented within a predetermined context, that picture will steer the conversation. Some have called this "the death of print", where images supplant reason by propagating themselves throughout the collective mind through the media, which has become ubiquitous in our daily lives. The pictures themselves have become the ideas, and they hold enormous sway over the general public. How? Because to get their ideas across, images require very little thinking.

It's no secret that the power of persuasion has risen to unprecedented technological heights. There are those who have discovered how to influence the collective mind for their own commercial interests, and science has given them ways to enhance their influence exponentially. There is nothing insidious about this; it's just what people do, especially when they have something to sell.

Ever since Sigmund Freud's American nephew, Edward Bernays, applied Freud's ideas about the unconscious mind to the techniques of modern advertising, the world's populations have been steadily nudged into becoming members of the culture of desire. By the manipulation of our basic human needs at the subconscious level, we have been trained to want things that are not in our best interest to want, and to want more and more of them. The collective mind has become the collective appetite, and rational self-interest has atrophied to the point where it is almost non-existent.

Persuasion has always existed in the human drama, but never like it does now. We are continually bombarded with images, colors, and sounds that trigger our deepest emotions, and we aren't even aware of the effect they are having on us. There are colors to stimulate our appetite, colors to calm us, colors to rouse and arouse. Colors are the subliminal context of the ads we see. Certain images, especially those that are taboo, draw our eye almost involuntarily, even more so when they are subtle. And sounds—a racing heartbeat in a scary movie, a baby's cry, a piercing, high-pitched tone— when combined with images and color can immediately capture our attention, whether we want them to or not. These elements make up the advertiser's palette. After all, the first rule in advertising is *get their attention!*

These techniques are not limited to commerce. They are also heavily used in politics. One of the best ideas to come down through history is Ancient Greece's idea of citizenship. It marked a turning point away from the rule of despotic kings and moved us towards the rule of law. It was a philosophical shift away from a warlord culture to a civil society, a true step forward in humanity's spiritual evolution. And though it may have only existed as an ideal, it is a worthy ideal. But it is not an ideal shared by everyone, especially not by those who have a deep distrust of people in large groups—the so-called "mob."

With the advent of democracy came a concerted effort to control the populace by subtle means, to get people to believe that they have a choice without actually having any choice at all. Because when choices are confined to a limited set of options, there is no freedom of choice. All you have is a set of options. Control the options, and you control the choices. This doesn't necessarily mean that there is a global conspiracy. It means that the collective mind has this limited set of options built into it. We are like rats in a maze—a maze we built ourselves.

Anyone with a modicum of knowledge about psychology can easily control others, simply by manipulating their basic needs. Those needs are enumerated as fight, flight, feeding, and fornication—the "Four Fs," all of which operate primarily at the unconscious level. By stimulating people's natural instincts towards anger, fear, avarice, and lust, and by doing it covertly so that no one realizes that they are being stimulated, you can create mass-movements that will serve your needs, not theirs. This is what drives the global economy, the primary beneficiaries of which are a few people at the top of a very tall food chain.

If the world's flow of money could be pictured as a global watershed, it would consist of three major rivers. The names of those rivers would be Prostitution, Drugs, and Guns. All other revenue streams would be tributaries of these three rivers. No one will admit this, of course, but it's not difficult to see that sex, pain-relief, and military force are written so large on this planet that their billboards can be seen from outer space. These are the main activities on

Planet Earth. They are the drivers of the rat race, and that other race—the human race.

Survival is our main concern, and no matter how comfortable we are in the moment, it lies just beneath the surface ready to spring forth at any moment. Know that about people, and you can lead them anywhere, get them to do anything, and turn them against anyone. But people aren't stupid, which is why it has to be done quietly. If you're too blatant about it, they will see that you're trying to manipulate them, and they will resist you with everything they've got. This is why politics and advertising are so inscrutable—changes have to be made slowly, quietly, and below the threshold of conscious awareness.

True power of persuasion does not reside in the message; it resides in the context within which the message is delivered. Therefore, much attention is given to shaping the contexts of the societies in which we live. For example, if the concept of "freedom" is presented within the context of a consumer culture, "freedom" will mean "freedom to spend." Within that context, it's easy to sell credit, because a lack of cash shouldn't get in the way of people's freedom to buy whatever they want. That way, even those who know that acquiring more debt is not in their best interest will do it anyway, because "freedom" is a right and is therefore moral. If a consumer is what you ARE, then taking on more debt is justifiable, regardless of how much it costs. It's the context of consumerism that controls the conversation called "freedom." The context has all the power.

Priests and advertisers are very much the same in that both are masters of context. The difference between them is that priests operate on the mental plane (the sanctuary), not in the media. It's not that we don't create videos and write books. We do. But to really get our message across, we go directly to our audience, not through their physical senses. When we speak, we speak existentially—we speak the Word. Then our message arises from within the individual, from an area that is deeper than the intellect, deeper even than the unconscious. How? By correlating our message with ideas in the Christ Mind, the source of the broadcast that forms and informs human being.

When we awaken to the reality of our mental environment, we see that we are never alone. We all occupy the same mental space with those who are connected to us in some way. It's as though we are in an auditorium standing in the middle of the floor, surrounded by people with whom we are most connected. Those with whom we have strong emotional ties are closest to us, regardless of whether they are related to us physically. Those with whom we are related to casually or through work are farther out. And those with whom we simply share the same nationality or ethnicity are farther out still. But we are in communication with all of these people, usually on an unconscious level.

The exact mechanism by which this takes place is not as important as are its effects. If the overall mood is one of anxiety, we will feel it, but we won't know *why* we're feeling it. And when we're feeling afraid, we are most susceptible to certain kinds of manipulation, such as accepting that terrorism is an imminent threat. Whether it actually is a threat is not the issue; accepting restrictions on our personal freedom and privacy is. It's not only firearms that float down the River Guns—it's tighter security measures and defense contracts as well.

If we develop our inner faculties to the degree that we are able to sense our psychic connections with other people, then we can begin to use those connections to affect the mood of the greater group. All we have to do is to be conscious of those connections while we engage in our spiritual activities. For instance, when we are at the altar performing a sacred rite, such as the Mass or Communion, we can include all those who are in our presence. We can let the energy of the grace flow through us to them. As long as we know that we are not the one who is "doing" it, no ill effects will come our way. We simply state our intention that this be done, and it will be. There is nothing magic about it. All God needs is a connection, and that is what we are here for. We set the pattern, and God takes it from there. God does the work.

I recently heard of a woman, a musician, who participates in a prayer group but who doesn't like to pray openly in that kind of setting. So instead of praying out loud, she plays a piece of music for the person being prayed for. We may not all be musicians, but we each have our own way of offering our intentions to the divine mind, whether it's through the act of approving a loan or baking a batch of granola. The kind of action is unimportant; it's the intention behind the action and the purpose for which (or for whom) the action is made that determines where the energy will flow. Altars and sanctuaries are symbols for inner realities. You can be anywhere doing anything and still invoke the presence and the power of God.

If we act in concert with other priests, our influence can be very powerful. But the agreement must be simple, not ideological. As long as no one is trying to convert people to their religion, get them to buy a certain product, or vote for a particular candidate, but rather approach them in the spirit of blessing, no harm will be done. And if you ever feel uncomfortable doing this, you can insulate yourself in your own inner sanctum, a practice you should develop anyway. We all have that place within us where no one can come except God. It is how we are when we are there that determines the quality (and the efficacy) of our presence in the world. This is the sum and substance of our priestly work.

Those who would control the collective mind for their own purposes have a vested interest in keeping the door to human potential closed, while our job as priests is to hold it open. The more spiritually free people become, the harder they are to manipulate, the harder it is to scare them, and the harder it is to get them to buy products they don't need. This is why the Priesthood is not a business but a service. The Gates of Heaven are free. No one should ever charge for admission. And demanding that people believe in certain doctrines or profess specific articles of faith is just another way to make them pay. But it's not as though anyone can prevent people from experiencing God. All they have to do is to get them to disqualify *themselves* by believing that they are unworthy sinners. True priests preach empowerment, not sin.

What I'm speaking of here will not make much sense if you haven't had certain spiritual experiences. My purpose in presenting these ideas is not to simply pique your interest, but rather to invite you to pursue this line of work. If you know that these things are real, then perhaps you will gain something from this discussion. If you have yet to experience these things, then maybe it will motivate you to begin a serious program of spiritual development. If your calling to the Priesthood is real, then such a program will help you to grow into greater and greater levels of service to God and the Host above. And as you spread your wings, they will provide the lift.

CHAPTER 27

REVOLUTION

We need a spiritual revolution. The priests of the world need to assert their authority and lead their respective religions towards a new vision of spirituality, one that includes all people everywhere, not just one group over another. We need priests who take their authority from a personal experience of the Divine and not from man-made institutions. We need priests who respect each other and support each other's work, regardless of which Book they read from or the clothes they wear. We need priests who know how to use the Word of Power, who know that what they bind on Earth is bound in heaven, and what they bind in heaven is bound on Earth.

We need priests who know how to get their prayers answered.

Revolution must also be evolution. In fact, why don't we just drop the "R" altogether and become evolutionaries? We can evolve instead of just revolve. Revolutions often come at a price. They tend to scrap too much of the past in favor of their own radical ideas. Sometimes, mostly by luck, they add one or two good ideas to the world discourse, but the mountains of destruction they leave in their wake are usually devastating. We have been going around and around this same old path for centuries. It's time we climb out of that rut, head straight for the summit, and claim it. Let us rejoice that there are an unlimited number of paths to the top of the mountain and support each other's attempts to get there, and not insist that everyone do it our way. WWII American general George Patton once said, "Never tell people how to do things. Tell them what to do, and they will surprise you with their ingenuity."

It would be a huge step forward if the spiritual leaders of the world could visit each other's houses of worship and participate in each other's rituals, each acknowledging the validity of the other's spiritual path. No one has to abandon his or her tradition; the different religions don't have to bleed into one amorphous "world religion." What would be the point? Since there is strength in diversity, let there be diversity. But, let there also be deep and genuine respect for those whose beliefs and practices differ from our own.

The question you should ask yourself, whether you are a priest or are seeking to become one, is this: Am I a priest for everyone or just those who look and think like I do? Am I a Christian priest, or am I a World priest? Am I sectarian, or am I a universal servant of God? These are enormously important questions. Unless the community of priests throughout the world—across all lines of demarcation, whether religious, political, or geographical—can unite in one, powerful, spiritual voice, the chances of humanity surviving with its hard-won civilization intact are slim to none.

Our common fate needs global cooperation like a jumbo jet needs a long runway. Once an A380 leaves the ground, it had better have a place to land. And our technology-based civilization is definitely airborne. But unlike an airplane, our civilization machine has the capacity to grow larger and larger while in flight. It has grown so large, in fact, that no runway exists large enough to catch it should it require an emergency landing. Our technological infrastructure is too big and too complex for us to turn back now. If it fails, billions of us will die, and all of the spiritual advances we have made will be lost. Forget about spirituality; people's highest aspiration will be simply to survive!

Everyone has a right to his or her political beliefs, even priests. But politics has deteriorated into "us against them," and a priest can never exclude anyone on the basis of their politics. *Our kingdom is not of this world.* Our role is that of mediator, not that of political or sectarian champion. We cannot advocate for the poor while at the same time demonize the rich. All people have a right to exist, not just the ones we like or with whom we agree. Those aspects of human nature that we find abhorrent will persist long after their current agents have died. They will surface like weeds wherever there is willing soil. It's the aspects themselves that are the enemy, not their human manifestations.

We have to internalize the realization that "there but for the grace of God go I." This doesn't mean we have to condone or turn away from horrendous acts. On the contrary, it invigorates us to fight the good fight. But it also keeps us from demonizing the other group. Demonization is the antithesis of compassion. From it have spawned all of our justifications for subjugating and committing violence against our fellow human beings. It is the utter rejection of the spiritual principle, "Love your enemy."

Why not eliminate the word "enemy" from our priestly vocabulary altogether and never use it publicly again? Instead, we could use the word "neighbor" whenever and as often as we can, so that the very concept of "enemy" would be eradicated from the collective mind. The worst atrocities are simply the manifestations of the suppressed negativity within the collective unconscious. They find their expression in those weakest links of humanity's chain of being. Any time someone in any part of the world gives in to thoughts and feelings of hatred and anger, it feeds the fires at the core of the collective mind, which in turn vent themselves through the first available crack. The real war, therefore, is the one inside of us—each and every one of us. This is the Holy War. And as priests, we are its knights.

There is a revolution taking place—an evolution. As priests, we cannot afford to take sides in the outward manifestations of social change. The problems facing the Earth today are so large and complex that no one group is capable of solving them. We are all in this together—rich and poor, religionist and atheist, white and "other." Our common ground is both literally and figuratively the very ground we stand on—the Earth! Let's work together with our brothers and sisters, whoever and wherever they are. Our life depends on it.

CHAPTER 28

LIGHT

Priests are practitioners of the world's Ancient Wisdom Teachings. This is our primary function. All the rest—the ministry, the counseling, building spiritual communities, etc.—is ancillary to this, our core mission. The mandate, however, is to use the world's Ancient Wisdom Teachings for the good of all, not to promote ourselves or advance one group over another. Our job is to save all souls, not just the ones we like.

Light is the presence of the power of God made manifest in our being. It's what makes it possible for us to see that part of God that lives within us. It also makes it possible for people to see God in everyone else, thus opening the door for true compassion. It's hard to attack someone when you see yourself in them. This makes light a priest's most effective tool in bringing heaven to Earth.

White light—Sunlight—has the entire spectrum of colors within it. Therefore, it can fill any need. Not only does it carry God's intelligence, it knows how to fill all the gaps. It knows, so we don't have to. All we need to do is open up and receive it. The more light we carry, the more we become channels for God's grace.

The power of the presence of God resolves all issues. Light is the manifestation of that power—and its vector. Light heals. It opens hearts. It makes forgiveness possible. When we carry the light, we become the door through which the power of God can flow into the world. And as it flows into the world, it automatically restores balance, both physically and mentally. The light brings peace.

Seeing inner light comes through deep relaxation—not sleep but the ability to relax while remaining conscious. Through deep relaxation, the light that is present in us turns inward instead of radiating out, and we become profoundly quiet. The silencing of our thoughts produces a vacuum, which then gets filled with more light.

Negative thoughts occlude the light, making it more difficult for us to see it. This is why we work hard to eliminate negative thinking. It is also why we work to eliminate it in the collective mind, so that the light, which is the presence of the power of God, can be made manifest in the life of the world.

It's important to remember that as these negative thought-forms are dislodged and begin to come out, we must not give them any life. Instead, we let them pass through our awareness without grabbing onto them, analyzing them, or thinking that they reflect who we are as a person. The same thing applies when we see the negative thought-forms coming up within the collective mind. We let them pass by. The fastest way to help them disappear altogether is to keep adding light. The slowest, least effective course of action we can take is to engage with problems at their own level.

We also have to remember how these negative thought-forms got here in the first place. We let them in! Therefore, it is our responsibility to get rid of them, and we do that by means of the energy generated by the presence of God, the same energy that lights our being. In order to do this, we have to recognize that the energy of life is good. We have to trust it before we can follow it through the corridors of our inner life.

It can be difficult to reach this level of consciousness on our own. We all need help, regardless of how spiritually evolved we think we are—help from our friends, from our teachers, and sometimes, perhaps, from a counselor. The only real mistake is to think that you can tough it out on your own. You cannot.

Since light—the Christ light—is the energetic manifestation of the power (life) of God, it has two major effects in our lives:

1. Light enables us to see. Sounds simple. But what's true in the physical is also true in the spiritual: *we need light to see.* Just as light reveals features of the physical world, it also reveals finer and finer aspects of the spiritual world. The more light, the greater the resolution. Inner light and outer light are two aspects of the one light. They only differ in their rate of vibration. As our brains develop the ability to see on the spiritual plane, the more sensitive they

will be to spiritual light. Meditation develops this ability, if you look for it.

2. Light also makes you more visible to others. The more light you take on, the more you will stand out, especially to those who have developed their spiritual vision. People with average development will sense that there is "something" about you, but they won't be able to discern what it is. Depending on their predisposition, this will either tend to make them trust you or it will make them suspicious. But it's the light that grabs their attention, not you necessarily. In those cases where someone might be attracted to you anyway, regardless of the amount of light you carry, the light will accentuate their attraction many fold. It's important, therefore, to be ethical in your relationships with others. Always set realistic expectations, and then stand by them.

The light will cause your negative thought-forms to rise to the surface of your awareness, or worse yet, cause you to act out unconsciously. That's why we need a wingman—someone who will say, "Hey, did you see that? Did you see what you just did?" That's usually all it takes to make the unconscious conscious, which is what counseling is all about.

If you practice them consistently, meditation and spiritual discipline will help you to get clear of the negative thinking you have acquired over a lifetime. But often the effect of such disciplines will cause a teacher to appear in your life; the difference that the exercises produce in your personal vibration will draw him or her to you, or you to them. They will see your light, and you will see theirs.

We are automatically attracted to that with which we resonate. But don't fall into the trap of thinking that just because someone impressive shows up that they are automatically the one. Don't be afraid to test them. If they are the right teacher for you, they will keep showing up, and it will be difficult for you to ignore them. And if they're not the right teacher and you follow them anyway, your intention will carry you through. After all, it's God you're seeking, not another human being, right?

One of the most common mistakes students make is in thinking that their teacher can do no wrong. Always remember that no matter how advanced a teacher is, he or she is still capable of making mistakes, sometimes *huge* ones. You have to allow them the space to be human. Just remember that you're not seeking someone to worship, nor should you allow someone into your life who wants to be worshipped. This can only be a recipe for disaster. Instead, look for someone who places the emphasis on the training itself, the same kind of teacher you would want if you were learning to play a musical instrument. Some music teachers, especially those who work with advanced students, can be hell if you're being lazy or careless. So don't judge teachers by how hard they are. On the contrary, the more they try to make you feel special, the more likely they are to abuse your trust later on. Look for those who are professional and who keep their relationship with you friendly but impersonal.

Qualified teachers know that the best way to keep your mind off of your problems (the problems that will arise as your self-awareness increases) is to keep you busy. In my own training, I was kept busy day and night doing everything from menial house chores to attending classes or taking care of homeless people. I scarcely had time to dwell on my problems. This is a very effective way to advance quickly, but not everyone has the opportunity to live in such a structured, spiritual environment. Just remember that the busier you are, the better. Don't start thinking that you aren't progressing fast enough. Get up and do something— anything. Prayer is also good. If you want to complain, complain to God. And if you need to yell, yell at God. He's a big boy—he can take it. The best prayers are those in which you say what you're afraid to say. Understand?

During this process, meditate. At first, you will probably fall asleep a lot, but that's okay. Just keep meditating. Soon you will feel the influx of power, and that's when it gets interesting enough to keep you awake. That's when you start to look for the light. As long as you don't try to run from it, the power will manifest as light as you let go to it. It's going to take trust on your part, so any thoughts of evil or demon possession (or any other nonsense that people like to scare themselves with whenever they start to become aware of the power within their own being) will only make you want to stop training. Just know that this is a threshold that every seeker has had to cross. Jesus had to, and so did Buddha. Each had their "temptations" that they had to overcome. And the biggest temptation of all is to run. Don't give up. Stick with it. Push through your fears.

What you are attempting to accomplish is completely natural. It's what humanity was made for. As spiritual beings, we are the agency through which the powers of God are made manifest in this world. Spiritual training is the process by which we become what we already are. It's not so much about learning ideas as it is learning how to use the power of God in your life. It's learning how to be the way God created you to be. It's only through negative thinking that we forget our true relationship to the All. Spiritual training undoes all that. Ideas are helpful, but it's power that does the work. Learn to be with the power, to let it move through you, and to use it in your everyday living.

Let's get clear about light. Throughout this book, we have been talking about the Son/Sun of God, how the Sun's light fills this Solar System, and how it not only conveys energy but also intelligence. The Sun is the source of all life. Without it, no life could exist on this planet. It is only through humanity's ability to think (to have thoughts) that people have convinced themselves that they are somehow separate from nature. And the churches, especially the Christian churches, haven't been much help in dissuading people from this mistaken belief. In fact, they have encouraged it. Consequently, we have a planet that is on the verge of collapse, both socially and environmentally, because people have separated themselves from the power of God that runs through all living things.

Here is the one thing to keep in mind when thinking about light: *light is life made visible*. The more conscious we are of the light of life, the more we can SEE it. All life radiates light, but it's invisible to the undeveloped eye. As your eyes become attuned to the light of life, you will begin to see it everywhere. Most importantly, you will see the Self, that which you truly are, the being whom God made you to be.

Some final thoughts: What we see, we see by light. As light is reflected off of a physical object, it reaches our retina and then our brain. But sometimes we don't see a thing, even though it is right in front of us. Why? Because we have no concept of it, as in the story of the Indians who could not see the tall ships moored right off their shore. It's the idea of a thing that causes us to look for it. In cases such as this, the light comes from within us. It shines outward upon the world seeking its corollary.

However, if the soul is troubled or undeveloped (susceptible to fear and pride) then the ideas are mere "projections," as that word is used in popular psychology. But if the soul is developed to the extent that it's able to access ideas from the higher mind, then the light that is projected outward from the individual is a spotlight, shining into the darkness in search of truth.

This is why meditation is so important, regardless of what field or discipline you are in. Because as you avail yourself to higher ideas, or shall we say "God's Mind," the more the true patterns of creation will reveal themselves to you, and you can put them to use in science or music or spiritual study, or whatever path you are on. But if you're satisfied with worldly interpretations of spiritual truths, then that's all you'll find, which is merely more of the same—those ideas that are manufactured for mass appeal. Therefore, let the light that is within you shine forth into the world. Let it be from the highest in you, the Christ in you. Be a channel of light.

AFTERWORD

Now that you have read *World Priest*, I would like to ask that you change your perspective. Instead of being on the receiving end of these ideas, become a vocal point for them. Get up from your seat in the back of the classroom and come up to the front, turn around, and face the world. Speak your Priesthood into the One Mind. Whether you do it out loud or silently with your thoughts, *be* the truth of your being. Take it on. Let your actions be the living symbols of your intention. If you hold a child in your arms, take a moment from time to time and let him or her stand in for *all* children. Let your love encompass all children everywhere. If you send money to a charitable organization, let it be a declaration of victory for the right and the good. When you show up for work, *be* the manifestation of economic prosperity and productive cooperation. And if and when you serve at the altar, *be the presence of God in the world.* Don't be afraid to let the Highest express Itself through you. After all, that is what the Priesthood is all about. Be a priest to the world. Be a World Priest!

ABOUT THE AUTHOR

Michael Maciel is a priest and master teacher of the Holy
Order of MANS. He was ordained into the priesthood in
1972 by Dr. E. W. Blighton (Father Paul) at the HOOM
headquarters in San Francisco, California.

In 2010, Michael was ordained into mastery by Master
Timothy Harris of the Gnostic Order of Christ in San Jose,
California. Since then, he has officiated and participated in
priest ordinations and rites of initiation.

Michael currently sits on the Board of Directors of the
Holy Order of MANS, a non-profit corporation in the State
of California.

You can read more of Michael's writings on the following
websites:

The Mystical Christ
www.mysticalchrist.org

Michael Maciel
www.michaelmacielauthor.com

Facebook
www.facebook.com/michael.maciel.3975

Michael is also the author of The Five Vows, Raising Your Spiritual Commitment to the Next Level, available on Amazon.

Printed in the United States
by Baker & Taylor Publisher Services